I Have Survived:
My 'Me Too' Story

Onjolee

I Have Survived:
My 'Me Too' Story

Vanguard Press

VANGUARD PAPERBACK

© Copyright 2023
Onjolee

The right of Onjolee to be identified as author of
this work has been asserted by her in accordance with the
Copyright, Designs and Patents Act 1988.

All Rights Reserved

No reproduction, copy or transmission of this publication
may be made without written permission.
No paragraph of this publication may be reproduced,
copied or transmitted save with the written permission of the
publisher, or in accordance with the provisions
of the Copyright Act 1956 (as amended).

Any person who commits any unauthorised act in relation to
this publication may be liable to criminal
prosecution and civil claims for damages.

A CIP catalogue record for this title is
available from the British Library.

ISBN 978-1-80016-447-5

*Vanguard Press is an imprint of
Pegasus Elliot Mackenzie Publishers Ltd.*
www.pegasuspublishers.com

First Published in 2023

**Vanguard Press
Sheraton House Castle Park
Cambridge England**

Printed & Bound in Great Britain

My mother, who has given me my life and my education with the sacrifices she made. She did her best with what life dealt her. I wish I could have looked after her then and had the means to do more for her now.

My son, who gives me hope and the responsibility to carry on.

My partner, for his love.

My sisters, they are unique.

Preface

This book, this memoir, is a labour of hope and new beginnings for me. It is also a testimony to how far I have come—from a young, innocent girl who was a helpless victim of child abuse to an adult who has faced numerous challenges that I have overcome. It is not easy to bare your soul to the world and let them in on your dark secrets. But I found the courage and inspiration somewhere deep, deep inside me. Each chapter of my memoir has been a journey of self-discovery. From the dark interiors of my mind and heart, I have exposed it all. These are my experiences, my feelings, my fears, my joys, and my despairs. You may have heard or read about thousands of other such incidents, yet I believe that you will find something new in this book, because the story is mine and I am not just a "me too" statistic. I am a part of this movement in blood, flesh, and tears. My story is mine; it's unique, just like each and every one of us is unique. And my story is life-affirming because in spite of all the darkness and turmoil, I have not only survived, but thrived.

Life has been inexorable, as life is for most. I have fought to meet it head-on despite my fears and self-doubts. I have shed copious tears while writing at times, while at others, I have smiled too. I wonder how I made it this far. I was crushed down to my soul over and over again, but somewhere, from within the dungeons of that all-enveloping darkness, I found the strength to carry on.

I have been holding onto this awful secret from when I was a little girl. I have walked the paths of life from school to college to marriage and motherhood with these horrible skeletons rattling in my cupboard. I hid everything and put up a façade of being confident and carefree so as not to hurt others. But it has been a massive burden and it has taken its toll on me and my relationships with others. My past haunted me like a ghost, an ever-lurking presence threatening to upend any happiness that I craved or experienced. But now, there are no regrets. If anything, there is this glorious sense of freedom from breaking out of the mould and in shedding the baggage of the past.

Both nature and nurture wronged me during my formative years. The mark left on me is permanent; there is no concealing it. The best I can do is to bare it all after having locked it away for so many years and take strength from the knowledge that my story is worth sharing. I do not blame anyone today, except the monster who changed the trajectory of my life for the worse. On some level, I believe I was dealt with this card by destiny. There's no point in indulging in what-ifs. I cannot change my past. It is there. It happened. I cannot daydream about having another life or being someone else, because that would throw me off track from tackling life in all its facets—be it good or bad. Life may have thrown a lot of challenges my way, but it has also offered me many precious gifts.

I hail from a small town in a remote state in India. My mother was a young widow who was also trying to navigate her way in the world. Her journey was harder than mine, steeped as she was in a patriarchal society without a man by her side to 'protect' her. She was forced to follow the rules set out by the so-called guardians of society and religion. If she had not been subdued, if there had been a father figure around me while I was growing up, would things have been different?

I was taught to live to please, instead of being taught to live my own life. Speaking up was not an option. Fear was drilled into me. What may set tongues wagging mattered more than what would make me happy. The impact of such nurturing was like teaching me to live on my knees, eroding my self-belief and leaving a lasting effect on the core of my being—to be submissive, subservient, and feel unworthy.

When I needed it most, I didn't get any support for the repeated abuse I faced. I never got a chance to get my voice heard or get justice. There was no one I could turn to, no one to support me. This, in turn, affected my mental well-being, resulting in mood swings and angry outbursts. I struggled to find equilibrium; I struggled to forge a new path and leave my sordid past behind. But the past would weigh me down, making me drown so many times. Fortunately, however much my weaker self would try to pull me back, my stronger side and the support of friends, my son, my therapist, spiritual guru, and my partner would lift me up. I am a small town girl who has come a long way. Today I am a single mother living in a foreign country and pursuing a successful career.

Even that was not handed to me on a silver platter. Diversity and inclusion were words I had not heard of then, in my early days in the UK. I had to give up my job to look after my son. The business needs of a large company were bigger than my needs. People and circumstances tried to take me down time and again, but I did not yield. Like a phoenix, I rose from the heap of ashes every time, renewed, refreshed, and raring to go.

If life has taught me one lesson, it is that problems will always arise. It's never going to be an easy ride. And for someone like me, with all the unimaginable, terrible baggage that I carry, it is even more difficult. But these magic words—never to give up—have stood me in good stead and will continue to anchor me and inspire me. Just like all those brave women who had the courage to tell their stories and out the abusers, this is my story of hope and resilience, my "me too" moment that I want to share with the world. If it provides hope, inspiration, or courage to even one person, I will be content. One more voice saying 'me too'; one more voice adding to the clamour to punish evil men who prey on women; one more voice that helps to take down the claustrophobic, limiting walls of patriarchy. Each and every voice counts and step by step, we all can make a change. That is my hope and my dream.

Chapter 1
Childhood in the Mid 1970s...

I was the girl who was meant to be a boy.

Yes.

Was that the beginning? Was my ill-omened birth a sign of what was to come? Of all the trials and tribulations I faced. Of all the evil I came face to face with.

Patriarchy looms its ugly head in almost every corner of the globe, but in India, we have elevated it even further. A girl child is not a welcome addition to a family. Unless they already have a son. Traditionally, most families want boys. The girl child is not greeted and feted with the same joy and exuberance and lively celebrations as the boy child is. In certain parts of India, female infanticide is very prevalent. It's changing with growing awareness and harsher laws, but the practice still persists. Sex selective abortions, although banned by the law, are the norm in many parts of the country. As per a 2018 report titled 'Female Infanticide Worldwide: The case for action by the UN Human Rights Council', India has among the highest female foeticide incidents in the world.

On a hot day in July, in the town of Guwahati in the north-eastern state of Assam in India, I was born.

Today, Guwahati is a sprawling city, but in the seventies, it was a picturesque town. Surrounded by the verdant Shivalik hills, with the mighty Brahmaputra River snaking its way through the town, the city has an undeniable charm to it. Thanks to the burgeoning population, the contours of the city have transformed. Today, the town is dotted with skyscrapers; it is more polluted and much hotter too. As summer draws to a close, the moisture-laden monsoon clouds are awaited. Once the monsoon hits, we get respite from the heat but now have to contend with relentless rains and flooding, which is an almost annual affair. The vast river provides both beauty and means of livelihood to the inhabitants of the state. In the crisp cool winter months, when the sand banks form, people picnic at these scenic spots, and some settlers also build temporary homes there.

Coming back to me, I was the seventh child (counting an unfortunate stillbirth) in my family. The sixth female. Instead of the much-awaited boy. After months of intense anticipation and prayers and *pujas*, I came into the world. Unwelcome. A pall of disappointment tainted the air.

From when my mother got pregnant with me, *Satyanarayana pujas* (special prayers) were performed every month, so that my parents would be blessed with a boy. A boy who would carry on the family name and provide security to my parents in their old age. A boy who would make them proud in a sea of female children. Alas, that was not to be.

Like most youngsters from conservative families in those days, my mother had been married off when she was just fifteen and became a mother at the tender age of sixteen. An age when she should have been studying in school, hanging out with friends, and enjoying a carefree existence.

Instead, she lived under the weight of expectations and the drudgery of domesticity; daily chores and looking after her husband and her family circumscribed and defined her existence. And to make matters worse, she was viewed as a failure because she was not producing the much-awaited boy child. In India, the burden of blame is always shifted onto the woman. The man is never to blame. It is the woman who has to carry the rock-filled sack of shame that will define her life, because conventional society looks down on you if you are unable to gift the world a boy.

And in my mother's case, she produced girl after girl. Her in-laws taunted her and pressurised her. They wanted a boy. Desperately. It was a matter of family honour. What would their standing be in society if their son could not become a proud father to a boy who would carry forward the family's legacy?

And so my mother was reduced to a baby-making machine, churning them out one after another in the desperate hope that the gods would be kind enough to grace her, and thereby the family, with a boy.

So on that blistering July day when I came into the world, our home and its surroundings were enveloped in a cloud of gloom. We lived in a modest bungalow in a large compound. My grandfather had owned the land and the houses within and had left them to his sons when he passed away.

The maid was waiting by the compound gate to pass on the news of my arrival into the world. With a huge sigh and a defeated expression, she would tell all those who enquired, "It's a girl again."

Thankfully, my father and my sisters were not weighed down by the disappointment that the extended family felt. My sisters were happy to welcome a new sibling into their home. They were too young to understand the undercurrents of the social expectations that had been dashed owing to my birth. For them, I was the new baby, someone to play with, to dress, to look after, and welcome into the folds of an already large family.

My father joyfully distributed sweets to family and friends to celebrate my birth. For him, it was a bittersweet moment. He was welcoming a new life while his own was slowly ebbing away, being ravaged on the inside by cancer. Life and death. The eternal cycle plays on. But at that point in time, there was a cruel irony to it all. A birth and an impending death. How fragile we are!

There was my mother with six daughters to look after. Not one. Not two. But six. Six 'burdens' that she would have to carry. Six 'burdens' who would need to be fed, educated, and married off. After all, in India, the ultimate goal for women is marriage. Once a woman is married and settled, her parents can heave a sigh of relief. Because they have got rid of the burden. In most communities in India, the dowry system is prevalent. It may be illegal but it still thrives. The bridegroom can ask for a fat sum of money as dowry or even demand it in kind—a car, a house, gold jewellery… And this is probably the underlying reason why people don't want girls. Saving up for dowry can be a daunting task, chipping away into a family's financial health. Whereas, if you have a boy, you are in a position of control. *You* ask for the dowry. The more qualified your son is, the handsomer he is, the fairer he is, the higher his caste… the more you can demand. Fortunately, in our community, we do not have the dowry system, so my parents didn't need to worry about saving towards that. Imagine having to shell out dowry for six daughters!

To this day, my mother has never told me how she felt on my arrival. Did she know my father was dying? Was there a deep well of disappointment within her? That she would not have a son to take care of her if anything happened to my father? Did she feel as if she had failed by producing one more girl child? Or did she accept it with equanimity? That this was her fate, her husband's fate. That they should have only daughters. Or did she look at me as a blessing? A sixth blessing?

Should I ask her? Will she give an honest answer? Well, there is no point in digging up the past now, is there? The dregs of the past, my mother's feelings on my birth, after all the *pujas* to appease the gods... maybe it's best left shuttered, a secret forever.

Because there's so much more melancholy that surrounds my birth.

You see, not only was I the girl who should have been a boy, crushing the weight of expectations with my arrival. But, I often mused, was my birth a bad omen? Is that why bad luck stalked me and those around me? Before I turned one, my father succumbed to cancer. My mother was left to pick up the shattered pieces after his death. She was alone in a man's world, alone with six female children...

My mother had had a difficult childhood. Being the eldest sibling, she was sent away from her family to her grandparents' home as they needed help. It must have been hard for her to live away from her parents and siblings. And to have to shoulder the responsibility of taking care of two old people.

The only silver lining in the murky clouds of her existence was when her father would go over to visit her. To date, she tells me how she used to look forward to her dad coming over. For a young teenager to have been plucked away from everything that was familiar, safe, and loving must have been bewildering and achingly lonely.

And before she could come to terms with her life away from home, she was married off. She was still a child, a young girl who should have been living a happy-go-lucky life. And then followed motherhood, at an age when she possibly needed mothering herself. Six children later, her husband dies. And she is a widow.

Life had thrown her one kick in the teeth after another. In India, widows are looked down upon. With changing social norms, they are no longer ostracized, but the journey post widowhood is one that is fraught with difficulty. In my mother's case, she at least had shelter because she had a home to call her own. But she was alone. She was not professionally qualified. She had never worked to earn a living. And in a society defined by patriarchy, she was a woman alone, with no man to protect her.

Life may have dealt her a bad hand, but my mother was made of sterner stuff. All the challenges she had faced in childhood and her marriage had shaped her into a woman of steel. Fortunately for us, we were not left in a financial hole. My father had left us enough for us to lead a comfortable life. My mother threw herself into managing the properties and land that father had left behind to provide for us, educate us, and get us married.

But navigating life without a husband can never be easy in a patriarchal and orthodox set up. Can a single woman protect her children from the evils that lurk around?

As I grew up, I realized that there was no safe cocoon. There was no escape from evil. There was nowhere to run. For many, family provides a safe haven, a ring of protection, where you stay snug and safe within its comforting folds. But for me, the ill-omened girl who was meant to be a boy, the family let me down…

Chapter 2
Present Day...

I'm on a beautiful Thai island. Dawn is breaking and the sea shimmers silver. As the sun comes up, the sea and sky are streaked with a riot of colours—purple, orange, red, crimson, and gold. Slowly, it turns balmy and the sunshine glows like golden butter, dispersing its warmth and lighting up the sea with gold-flecked waves.

I am staying at a picturesque private resort in this gorgeous tropical paradise. I have been fortunate enough to have been invited to stay here. I feel blessed.

I wake up early every morning to soak in the beauty of nature, to spend some quiet me-time, to enjoy the soothing sound of the waves as they lap against the sun-dappled beach. I sit alone, cross-legged on the golden sands, to practise some mindfulness and meditation. To connect with myself, to let go of the past. The waves playfully dash around me in complete abandon... Sometimes I feel the same way too.

Sitting there, in the midst of nature, with sea, sand, and sky around me, I can laugh and feel joy. I can relax. I can let go of myself. I can feel happy. I look at the distant horizon. It seems to embody the infinity of life, the endless possibilities. There is something beyond that horizon. It beckons me with hope, with yearning, with anticipation. Maybe there is a better future beyond that horizon, the promise of something new, something fresh, cleansed from the past. If there had been a multihued rainbow streaking across the sky, I would have believed that the mythical pot of gold would have been waiting for me across the blurred edges where the sea and sky meet.

The joy bubbles up inside me, threatening to overflow and subsume me. I am so happy that I am almost scared of losing the moment. Will it slip away like sand through my fingers?

This fear is something I have found hard to shake off. Even in my happiest moments, it lurks in a corner of my brain, a dark shadow, a grey cloud that threatens to obscure the sunshine, something amorphous that skulks around, waiting to plunge me into the gloom of darkness.

I remind myself of what my spiritual leader continually tells me. She has always advised me to tell myself that I'm a strong, loving, peaceful, and happy soul. She changed my life, helping me to heal and deal with all the darkness within me. I encountered her at a time when my life was in shambles, when I was a mess, my life a complete turmoil. She opened her heart and home to me. She was compassionate, loving, and reassuring. She made me feel I was human, whole, and worthy of love and life.

The sun is warm and the sea glitters like gold with diamond-tipped waves, but I feel cold inside. I look around at the beauty around me and try and shake of the cloud of foreboding that is obscuring the warmth. I tell myself… "Come on, life is good now, and everything is as it should be. I have a caring life partner and a son I adore, and they both, in turn, love and adore me. I have a stable occupation. I like what I do for a living, and my work is vastly appreciated. I have it all—love, a successful career, and financial independence. Yes, it seems like a dream for me, although friends and family say I deserve it all. They tell me it's time I enjoy and appreciate what I have." And I do, I really do. But… There's always a but… That small niggling doubt that turns into a grey haze, which turns into dark storm clouds that rage within me.

I know I'm blessed to know, feel, and experience the essence and beauty of what love really is. It's a gift, a gift only a few have. There must be a God, I suppose. After all that I've been through, I found out the true meaning of love with my partner, even though it was late in life. He is my rock, my anchor, and my admirer. He knows me and understands me more than I do myself. And accepts me for who I am, warts and all. Unlike me, he had a secure childhood with emotional stability, which he believes has shaped him to be who he is today, a man comfortable in his own skin, a man who is mature, stable, and loving.

As a mother my only prayer is that I can provide that same kind of stability and love for my son. He is the essence of my life and my responsibility. I live for him. I want to bring joy, constancy, and purpose into his life. I want to instil values in him. I want to see him grow up into a mature, responsible, compassionate individual. I want him to be a good man. It's that simple. If that happens, I know I would be a success as a mother.

As I sit on the seashore in this paradise in Thailand, I open my eyes and look around me. On the outside everything appears to be perfect. Nature has laid out a stunning vista for me to absorb and appreciate. Life is perfect. I have everything.

But... As I said, there's always a but, that pall of gloom that slowly moves in to shroud my joy. Yes, life is beautiful, but... Only I know that there is one part of me I wish I never had to live with. A part that is as black as those clouds. Murky, multifarious, dirty. Lurking in the background like a mammoth spectre, threatening to eclipse any joy I derive from my life.

But then I shake off the clouds. A sliver of light breaks through the darkness. I have come this far, and I thank God for giving me a strong spirit. For giving me the strength to fight, to forget, to forge ahead in spite of all the challenges that life threw at me. I kept falling, but I'd bounce back again. Like one of those toys, which bounces back every time after being punched down.

Yes, I should believe in my strength more often. I need to stand firm, I need to defeat the shadows that threaten to consume me and plunge me into their darkness. I am privileged in so many ways. Even though my father passed away when I was barely a year old, leaving my mother to shoulder the burden of bringing up six daughters on her own, my mother never gave up. She is an amazing woman, a woman of steel. I am fortunate that she gave me an excellent education, sending me to the schools and universities that I wanted to go to. I was the only daughter to be educated in a private convent, the best education one could find at that time in a small town like Guwahati. My mother lived frugally, sacrificing her own needs and putting those of her daughters first. And to save up for me to study at prestigious institutions like a convent school and a university in Mumbai (Bombay in those days), she would buy groceries with her ration card (a government initiative whereby families get subsidised rice, sugar, flour, and other staples).

When I was a kid, there was a consensus among the adults that I was bright child. Possibly something of a blessing for the special prayers and *pujas* that were performed when I was a foetus. It boggles the mind to digest the ludicrousness of it all. How could they not know that the sex of the child is, in most cases, fixed at conception?

Anyway, I think I did pretty well in school, making it worth my mother's while for all the sacrifices she had made. However, university was not a breeze, and I can't, with all honesty, say that I performed at optimum levels. Or did I? I am filled with so much self-doubt and am prone to self-criticism. I hold myself up to very high standards, so I personally feel that I could have done better. But more on that later…

With Father gone, life was never easy. And since I was the girl who should have been a boy, and the last child, my mother never got the much-longed-for son who should have provided her security and looked after her. My father left us, or should I say that he was snatched away cruelly from us. Our protector and our provider was taken away, just like that, and life, for the rest of us who lived on, would never be the same without him.

I hate the word 'cancer', because it was that evil disease that took my father away, robbing him of life and robbing us of a father. Ironically, Cancer is my star sign. Life has a funny way of hurling things at you, doesn't it?

Talking about hate, I have often been told that I need to learn to love myself. My spiritual advisor, my friends, and my family have encouraged me to do so. I wish it were that easy. When life constantly bombards you with obstacle after obstacle, when life forces you to come face to face with evil when you are young, innocent and vulnerable, when life snatches away a parent, leading you to lead a life of deprivation, when life isolates you, fills you with shame, fear, and dread…

how do you love life or love yourself? I have realized that I need to love myself if I want to be happy and at peace. But it's an uphill task and I am still learning how to. Maybe that's why I do not like my own company. I am scared to be alone. That's when the dark demons in my mind plague me, taunt me, make me feel worthless. The fog swirls around me, turning into threatening billows that plunge me into despair.

You may think I'm being some kind of martyr. Or that I'm wallowing in self-pity. Do read on to dispel the doubts you have, because this book is about my journey, a journey I've embarked on to reveal the dark secrets that still have their hold on me. Secrets that have shaped me. Secrets that will shock you. Secrets that have made me weak yet made me strong.

Now that I have decided to unveil my life, lay it bare, with all the flesh torn away to reveal the bones, I know that this journey is not going to be a cruise or a fun trip. As each memory is carefully plucked out from my brain, it sears me, pricks me, and I double over in pain and shame.

But I know one thing. I'm not a weakling any more. I will not give in to the shadows. I want to banish them from my life forever. Cleanse myself. Heal myself. And in the process, provide hope and succour to anyone who has experienced anything similar. I am a fighter, and I've always strived to do my best. I want to share my journey of how I've learned, and am still learning, to be my own best friend and enjoy my own company. The clouds are lifting and molten sunshine is piercing through the fog spreading comforting warmth, like a snug blanket. And that light and warmth gives me the courage and hope to keep moving forward and bring hope and sunshine into other people's lives.

Chapter 3
The Darkest Years...

I'm four years old... little more than a baby. Young, trusting, a blossoming flower, its soft petals just opening up to the realm around it. An innocent child with rosy cheeks who is just discovering the world, running around on plump legs to explore the treasures of life—the flowers, the garden, the skies. A child for whom life is magical. Who believes in fairies, pixies, elves. Who loved dolls and toys. A child cocooned at home with six older sisters who she looks up to, imitates. A child who follows her mother around devotedly. A child. An innocent little child.

And then the horror began. The horror that shaped the narrative of my life. The horror that forever ruined the concept of childhood. From age four, I realized that the world is an ugly place. A dangerous place. A place of shadow and light, where the shadows seemed to creep around in the corners, ready to obfuscate the light. Life was no more a song and dance for me. It was no more about idle curiosity... about taking innocent pleasure in seeing a beautiful flower in the garden or playing with a tattered doll. Or knowing that even if the sun set today,

I'd awake to a bright new morning of fresh possibilities, of new adventures, of novelty, of new-fangled experiences. No, the sun's bright light had been tainted, shadowed. The sun's golden rays could never bathe my world in a life of glowing possibilities any more. Because, each morning, I now woke up to shame, to fear, to a darkness that had engulfed my heart and my very being. Could the lustrous sunlight overshadow that darkness? Never. My own fragile light had been snuffed out.

My childhood, my precious childhood had been cruelly snatched away from me. How could I jump out of bed joyfully each morning to embrace a new day, to play innocently with my sisters, to know undiluted happiness? As a child the world is a tantalizing rainbow of possibilities. Yes, we fall and hurt ourselves. We cry and move on. Yes, we get scolded, yes we fight with our siblings, but once we are done with the distress, we move on. Because, the world is an oyster, and we need to dig out all those pearls. Run around free, living in the moment, unfettered by worry, welcoming the enchanted world of possibilities out there.

But when your life gets shattered, torn apart, ruined by someone you trust, how do you, as a tender four-year-old, navigate a world that now looms above and around you, fraught with danger and blackness, the light smothered by an evil that you never imagined, never even knew?

And when that evil presents itself in the shape of a loved one', a trusted relative, can you ever have faith in the world? Can you ever trust again? Can you look at the world with rose-tinted glasses? Never.

My father was gone. Here we were, a family of seven females, navigating a world built on the deep foundations of patriarchy. I, of course, was too young to know that. So we looked up to him, the revolting monster, who came cloaked in the garb of a saviour. Someone who had taken on the mantle of looking after us, the family without a man at its helm.

And the monster took full advantage of our vulnerability, of our trust.

How could I begin protect myself when I didn't even know what was happening? When it started happening, I was so confused. Bewildered. Was this an act of a love between an adult and a child? Then why did it feel so odd? Why was it so secretive? So hush-hush?

My little child's brain was trying to wrap itself around what was happening. I didn't know what sex was, let alone child sex abuse. I innocently though this was an act of love. But it did feel deviant, strange, and uncomfortable.

My little mind raced with an array of confused thoughts. Should I tell Mother? But Mother adored him, looked up to him. She depended on him. My sisters loved him. So, was there something wrong with me?

Was I reading too much into all this? Maybe I had done something wrong and I must be at fault.

And how was I to describe what had happened? Did I even have the vocabulary for it? And if it was an act of love from a man the family revered, then I couldn't be ungrateful, could I?

But deep down, I knew it was wrong. Even as children, our instinct kicks in. We know. But we don't know. We know that being touched in that way, surreptitiously, is not normal, it's not right. But we've also been taught to trust and respect our elders. So we wonder whether there is something amiss with us, with our reactions. After all, we are young, navigating a world where adults have set the boundaries, the rules, and the framework for reality.

So, our reality changes. The boundaries blur. The rainbow has disappeared. Now it is shades of black and white, with a leaden landscape of grey in between. But where are the lines between black and all those shades of grey? Do they even exist? Can we see past them and trace out a clear line? No, we can't. Our little minds are too overwhelmed in coping with this new reality. Of seeing our kaleidoscopic world of innocence and hope being transformed into one that lacks colour or dreams. Yes, we live in a child's body, but our innocence and sunny optimism have left us forever, plunging us into a monochromatic world devoid of trust.

My child's mind would ask myself, "Why does he do this to me?" I could not talk about it to anybody. I was scared of disrupting the smooth harmony of our lives. I was fearful about upsetting my mother and my sisters.

But most of all, I felt shame. That shame engulfed me inside out. I could never get it off me. It lurked within me, swamping me, defining me, changing me. It is a baggage I carry with me. Whenever I was challenged, be it on a personal or a professional level, I felt I was not good enough, it was all my fault. I was let down by my mind often, which spiralled into the vicious cycle of self-doubt and self-deprecation. If I could not find a solution or my answer was wrong, it meant I'd failed. This is where, over time, cognitive behavioural therapy (CBT) has helped me. My doctor advised me to check out this newly popular therapy. I was lucky to click with my therapist, and she helped me find a middle-ground and practice self-assertions of my own talents and positive attributes. If I didn't share this, I'd feel I've failed readers or fellow sufferers to find a way out of not being able to find self-worth.

I hated myself. There had to be something wrong with me. Otherwise why would the monster do this to me? Only me...

Life had changed so drastically. Now I was overcome with fear. Whenever he visited, I was scared. Would he do those unspeakable things to me? Would I have to endure his wickedness again? Would he paw me, touch me, stroke me? Would he put his dirty, filthy hand into my private parts and explore me? Would he squeeze my non-existent breasts? Would he sear my smooth soft flesh with his rough probing hands? Whenever it did happen, I would succumb, bile rising in my throat, but too scared to resist or scream. I would squeeze my eyes shut and pray… to a God who never ever listened to or answered the prayers of a desperate child besieged by a monster. I would hope that Mother or one of my sisters would come along and catch him in the act. I would fantasize about how they would scream at him, maybe hit him, and throw him out, with a dire warning to him to never ever step over our threshold again.

I had never missed my father more. Would this have ever happened if he was alive? Would the monster have had access to our home and us if Father was there? I'm quite sure he wouldn't because we wouldn't have needed a 'protective' male figure if we'd had Father. My mother would not have needed the monster's help.

The abuse continued well into puberty. In our teenage years, our awareness is so much stronger and we are also at a stage in life when we are so sensitive. We are in that fluid space between childhood and adulthood, exploring the world and its possibilities, and also becoming aware of our growing sexuality.

He kept treating me like an object at every opportunity he got. He would pull the neckline of my dress to look at my breasts and compliment me on how well they were growing. I felt shame, hatred, and self-loathing. I begged him to leave me alone. Then I started threatening him that I would tell everyone. The monster would just smile... a malevolent, smug smile. His position in the family and society was strong, unshakeable. He had power, position, and a sterling reputation. What chance did I have?

Even before I reached puberty, he used to talk to me about porn movies. I was a child. I didn't even know what blue movies were. And this depraved brute was telling me about movies where people had sex on screen. What kind of a degenerate beast was he? He wasn't satisfied that he had ruined my childhood, that he had taken away my agency, that he was sexually abusing me. Now he wanted me to watch porn. In his dirty, disgusting way, he told me that everyone did it, that it was perfectly natural. But in his sick head, it didn't register that I was not an adult and that our relationship, for want of a better word, was not consensual.

And what appalled me the most is that after puberty, my body reacted to his touches. I didn't understand why. I was filled with shame. Disgusted at myself. How could my body betray me like this? How could it respond to the touch of a monster? What kind of a person was I? I could scrub myself raw when I bathed, but the shame clung to me, refusing to get washed off. I felt sick to the core. I was filled with self-loathing. This dark, horrible secret was taking its toll on me. A fog of confusion surrounded me. I could only begin to understand my body's treachery recently when

I started therapy. My therapist explained to me that our body parts respond as they are meant to when stimulated, thereby getting aroused. It was not connected to the mind. It was pure instinct. Human instinct. It was not my fault that I was getting aroused.

When I was in my early teens, he started propositioning me to sleep with him, to have sex with him. He would reassure me that he would use protection, so I need not worry. I was still young and naïve. I didn't understand what protection he was talking about. How could he protect me when he was abusing me? He was the person I needed protection from.

I dreaded being sent to his house during my summer holidays. I always wondered how and why his wife did not notice what was going on. Or did she? Was she scared to upset the applecart and walk out on him? I think his neighbours knew, as a girl my age, who used to come and play with me, stopped coming one summer. He must have sexually harassed her, and she must have told her parents. Why did her parents not call him up? Why did they not confront him? Why did they not get him arrested? Because in a deeply patriarchal society, everyone fears that the girl will be blamed and the family will be shamed. The girl becomes impure, a stain on her family and society while the perpetrator goes free. Once her 'good name' has been tainted, she will never find a husband. And in India, that is the ultimate aim for every parent—to find a 'good' husband for their daughter. Then the burden is off the parents. It becomes the husband's duty to 'look after' the daughter. She is no longer their responsibility. And for the 'impure girl', it is even worse if she has sisters. Even her sisters won't find husbands because the entire family's name is polluted by this. This is the reality of Indian society. It's all about honour, about hollow outward appearances. People are more worried about what other people will say than about protecting their vulnerable daughters. So, if a daughter is sexually assaulted, it lies buried within the family, a dirty secret that has to stay hidden from the world, no matter what harm it is causing to the girl. All that matters is the outward appearance of normality. And the unblemished reputation of the girl. After all, she has to be a virgin if she wants to find a 'good' husband.

As I write this chapter, my body is tense, my chest is tight, and my hands tremble. All these years later, the past still has power over me. Yes, I've changed, I've forged a life path for myself... and I've transformed. But when I let my mind wander back to those dark times, even today, the hot shame of what happened courses through my body.

This fear lives in me even today. The formative years are very important as to how an individual shapes up while growing up. My formative years turned me into a being who feared everything; my subconscious always tried to find a negative 'what if'—what if I lose this invaluable friendship, what if something bad happens to my career. I am lucky to have found myself outside of India, where there is support and help for the likes of me. Instead of being shunned, I was embraced. Instead of saying I was worthless, I was shown to acknowledge and know my worth. I was taught to stand my ground and corner without the fear. I learnt how to depend on my own resources to deal with life's challenges.

No child should ever have to go through this. Sadly, so many do. Even today. Let down by adult monsters who win their trust and proceed to scar them for life. I never thought I'd ever be able to put this down on paper. To confess about the shame I've carried within me all these years. To be able to detail what that monster did. But I have evolved, I have healed (though I may never heal completely). And I know one thing with unshaking certainty. It was *not* my fault. I was let down—by the monster, by my family, by the eco-system I inhabited. And that's why I sit here today, writing this. Pouring myself and my heart out onto paper. It is a cathartic process for me. I am facing my monster. I am bringing up everything and regurgitating the past, summoning up the courage to face it, write it, record it, and, more importantly, share it. Because I know there are so many of you out there who may be holding a dark secret similar to mine within you. Letting it weigh you down, preventing you from living. And there are so many children out there, precious little innocents who right now, at this moment, are being assaulted by sexual predators—their parents, relatives, family friends, neighbours, priests, teachers... the list is endless.

Having a son of my own, I know I would be gutted if the same thing happened to him. I would do anything to save him from what I went through. And I wish, I really wish, this would never ever happen to another child as long as I'm alive. But I know the world has evil people. And this cycle perpetuates. This book is my way of helping others. Helping those who have suffered child sex abuse. I hope my story resonates with them and I hope they can heal and make themselves whole again. And I want to help parents and children by sending out a message. Parents need to *always* trust and protect their kids and give them utmost support. In a world where the spectre of evil lurks everywhere, you need to be vigilant. You brought this innocent child into the world. It's your duty to protect him or her.

I would kill anyone who dared harm my child. Today, I am an adult and when I look back at the monster who turned my childhood into a nightmare, I know he was not only an abuser of trust, a sexual predator, but also a paedophile. I know, in a civilized world we should hope the law will take its own course. But personally, I honestly wish he could be stoned to death in public. This treatment would still not be enough for his actions. So much for healing, huh? I told you, it never goes away. We learn to deal with it, cope with it and find happiness in our lives, but the past is there, just below the surface. If you scratch it, the wound surfaces and the anger and shame bubble up all over again.

I am the girl who was supposed to be a boy. Why, oh why wasn't I born a boy? Maybe then, the monster would not have fixated his depraved eyes on me…

Chapter 4
The Forbidden Narrative

Child abuse is still a taboo topic in India. Thanks to the media, cases do get highlighted, but that is only the tip of the iceberg. Even today. It's a territory that conservative society is loath to explore, discuss, or uncover.

And when I was growing up, it was unthinkable to have a conversation about it, let alone mention it.

It was something to be brushed under the carpet. It was something to be hidden. It was something never to be talked about. It was an evilness that existed, but it remained invisible even though its presence was an unwholesome reality.

After all, in India, as I mentioned in the last chapter, everything was about family honour. That had to be preserved at any cost. It was more important to present a façade of normality than tend to a young child who was being sexually abused. Especially if it was a family member who was the perpetrator. In that scenario, it had to be kept under wraps, irrespective of the damage it was doing and would do to the abused child.

And what makes me angry even today is that the abusers face no consequences for their heinous crimes. The abused live in shame because, when people come to know about what happened to them, they will be tainted and considered impure. In different parts of India, different cultures and religions deal with such situations in different ways. But there is one common denominator to this sad saga: the person—the victim whose life has been shattered, who needs the support most—does not get it. Instead, society works against them. Society shames them. Society isolates them. The victim lives—or rather exists—in a claustrophobic cloak of ignominy.

For parents of the victim, in most cases, especially when the victim is a girl, their only worry is that no one will marry into the family. After all the girl has been 'dishonoured'. She has brought shame into the family.

And in my case, the situation was made worse by the fact that we had no male member in our family. And six girls to marry off. In India, the girl child is considered a burden. The only aim of parents is to get their girls married into 'good' families, so that they are 'settled'. Then the burden is off them. Once married, the girl now becomes a part of her husband's family. She is no longer the responsibility of her parents. She belongs to her husband. It's patriarchy at its worst, stripping the girl or woman of any agency. She is not a person in her own standing. She is someone's daughter or someone's wife. That is her place in society; that is the space she inhabits.

And my evil abuser knew that. He knew that the family's honour was more important than what I was going through. He knew of the consequences I would bear for the rest of my life if I outed him. This is the reason, I believe, he kept going; he knew nothing could touch him while he could get his hands on anything, literally. He could continue with his abominable deeds with impunity. He was a male, a powerful one at that, in a deeply patriarchal society.

In later years, when I went to a healthcare professional, I was shocked by some examples he shared with me of how little girls in Indian villages get abused by brothers and fathers. The stories he told me made my stomach turn. Imagine how depraved patriarchy and society can be that young girls get abused by their own family members—their fathers and brothers. The people who should protect them are the ones who abuse them. They have no escape, nowhere to turn to. The evil lurks in their own homes and the perpetrators are their own flesh and blood. What future did these helpless young girls have? Who could they turn to? Where could they go? Nowhere. They were trapped. And once they reached 'marriageable age', they would then probably be married off to a man who would beat them up after drinking. That is their fate.

Such is the value of a woman; she is seen as meat by the flesh hungry, a mere sexual object, even by her own siblings and father, the ones who should actually be her protectors instead of preying on her. When a woman starts life with such a disadvantage and faces the iniquities of sexual abuse when she is an innocent child, she starts feeling different from others; she feels isolated, she feels unworthy, she tries hard to please, and aspires for success academically or in anything she undertakes in order to find a purpose in life. I know because that's what happened to me. Through no fault of mine.

People always say the world is unfair. And for me, after the nightmarish childhood I went through, I agree wholeheartedly. Unfair doesn't even begin to sum it up. There is no justice. To me, justice is a meaningless word; its scales are tipped in favour of the oppressor. The more powerful and the richer he is, the more he can escape any judicial scrutiny and get away with any crime.

Over the years, due to exposure to western media and the digital world that connects the world, the topic of physical abuse against children and adults has come to the forefront. The Catholic Church and the sex abuse scandal surrounding it has made headlines across the globe. Men of God, who pious believers entrusted their children to, betrayed that trust in the worst way possible. The scandal became an epidemic with hundreds of victims coming out to tell their stories. As more and more skeletons tumbled out of the closet, the world woke up to the horror and reality of child sex abuse and how prevalent it was. And as victims began to speak up about their experiences and share their trauma, people began to understand the true depths of horror and degradation that a child sex abuse victim suffers.

I guess that was why I felt I should write about my ordeal and share it with the world. Because today, people are more aware of CSA and are more empathetic towards it. However, when I sat down to write my story, it wasn't easy. I drowned under a seesaw of conflicting emotions... So many questions ran through my head. *How can I expose a family secret? Am I letting Mother down? Will I be ruining the family?* I know there are many who've suffered like me and even more than me; the pain, hurt, and shame cannot be compared because each case is unique. But the bruises left by this agony and suffering are similar. The bruises may heal on the surface but live deep in our hearts, however normal we try to appear to the world. Our outer world can be sunny and happy but our inner worlds are steeped in sorrow and shame and are surrounded by darkness.

In the process of grappling with and coming to terms with what happened to me, I read stories of other survivors and books by mental health professionals. And in the process, I identified common traits that all we CSA victims have. Some of them are self-doubt, a feeling of worthlessness, the inability to find a purpose in life, reliving those awful moments, suffering from a debilitating fear that something bad is going to happen, and a fear that what we have going well for us will be taken away too. Our minds are in a constant loop and the predominant emotion that overcomes us is self-blame.

I realized that it was only I who could help myself. And I so badly wanted to heal. As a result, I started examining what was available in the form of therapy. It was a long process. Initially, I tried almost everything from meditation to counselling and medication. But counselling wasn't helping me in any way. After my counselling sessions, I would be back to how I was. I wasn't healing. I was stuck in that dreadful loop. The dark clouds still enveloped me.

I needed something else. I started researching other forms of therapy. Over time, and I'll touch upon this again later, I realized there were no quick fixes. It was going to be a long journey of self-realization and self-discovery. After all the trauma that I had been subjected to from my childhood to my adolescence, the healing process was not going to be something that could be achieved in a jiffy. There was so much I had to learn and imbibe in order to heal and move forward. The most important thing I needed to do was to believe and understand that it was not my fault. I also realized that the strength to forgive and to move on is intrinsic to the process of transformation.

And even after all the therapy, to this day, I can so easily be pushed back into the abyss. I am shaken very easily. Those dark thoughts are embedded in my psyche; they've left a scar on my heart. This is when I remind myself of the techniques that I was taught by my therapists. I then consciously bring my mind back to the present, to the here and now. I remind myself that I am safe, I am strong, I am grown up, and I have a loving partner who supports and nurtures me. Yes, I have so many blessings in my life. But the shadows of the past so often obscure them.

I tend to take things personally and if things do not go right for me in my personal or professional life, I blame myself. Every so often, I have to remind myself that it was not my fault, cognitive behavioural therapy (CBT), which has become very popular these days, has helped me find the right strategies to cope and overcome in my moments of despair. When I started CBT, I did all the exercises diligently, as if to tick all the right boxes. But my heart was not really in it. As a result, obviously, I didn't reap all the benefits. It was only when I returned for further sessions—after a year or so—that things started making sense.

I realized how effective it was when I could apply the learnings of CBT to my experiences. This especially helped my thought process and my outlook on life. Life didn't have to be black, gloomy, dreary, or hopeless. My outlook on life became more nuanced and I was able to see shades of grey in between all that blackness. I also learnt so much more. I learnt not to misinterpret small actions and think that I was at fault. For example, I started realizing that if someone didn't greet me in the office it was not because of something I had done; it could be for numerous other reasons. I didn't have to take the weight of their behaviour on my shoulders and burden myself with thoughts that I had done something wrong or I was unlikeable. I wouldn't blame you for thinking that this comes naturally to most people. But owing to all the trauma I'd gone through and my lack of self-worth, I tended to believe that anything adverse that happened in my interactions with people was always my fault. When I started reading about how the trauma and stress an abused person goes through change the way we see and feel things, I chide myself for being so self-judgemental.

After facing the dread and shame of physical and verbal assault for over fourteen years, I wanted to escape from the claws of the evil relative. I told Mother I wanted to study in a big city. The monster did his level best to stop Mother from sending me off, saying girls should be at home as it was not safe to send them alone to a big city. He wanted me there so he could continue to abuse me. And I wanted to escape from there to stop the abuse.

I was no longer a child; I had a mind of my own. And I knew I had to get away from his malevolent clutches. It was difficult, oh so difficult, but I somehow mustered up the courage, God knows how, to tell Mother and my sisters what he had been doing to me.

Today, when I look back and ruminate on that day, there is an ache within me. They didn't believe me. They merely brushed me off, saying he was only being affectionate towards me. They simply wouldn't or couldn't see it or accept it. I was not surprised at their reaction. But I felt lost, betrayed, and bereft of the love and understanding I had believed would come from them. They were women, all older than me, more mature than me, more worldly-wise than me. Why could they not see what I had been through? Why could they not understand my pain?

Did they really believe that his behaviour was acceptable? Or did they think he had the right to do what he did?

These questions swarmed in my head. A fog of confusion enveloped me. And the pain of betrayal from the people I loved the most was not just painful but heart-breaking. I felt a kaleidoscope of emotions—numbness, anger, grief, pain, betrayal, hopelessness. I was devastated, an emotional wreck. I felt all alone in the world—unloved and untrusted. I had shared my deepest darkest secret with my family, anticipating that they would rush to comfort me, support me, and shower me with love and understanding. Instead they had forsaken me, betrayed me.

I cried for hours, screaming and shouting out to the neighbours to come and rescue me. No one came even if they may have heard me. I recall how my cheek smarted from the slap that Mother gave me for being brave enough to finally report him after so many years of being subjected to sexual abuse.

For Mother, all she cared about was society and what people would say—typical Indian mentality in those days. As far as she was concerned, I could not bring shame upon the family. No one would marry my sisters due to the disgrace and dishonour that I would bring upon the family. Yes, *I* was a disgrace. Not the monster who had destroyed my childhood by his evil acts. Through the lens of a patriarchal society, all the blame rests on the woman, even if she was robbed of her agency as an innocent child.

Today, after years of therapy, soul searching, and all the positive benefits I've reaped from cognitive behavioural therapy, I forgive Mother. She too is and was a victim of patriarchy. Her life and views of the world were shaped by it and she didn't know any better. She was herself not much older than a child when she had her first child. I take comfort in the fact that she loves me. To me, that is what is important. Yes, her reactions were abnormal, some may even say cruel. But in her reality, holding her own in a world dominated by men, and without a husband by her side, this was her way to protect her family. Unfortunately, I was the collateral damage.

Chapter 5
Light and Dark

Sometimes I wonder why I am penning this book. It brings back a surge of memories that consume me with grief and anger. Writing this book is not easy. I have to keep stopping, pausing, taking breaks, because otherwise I feel that I will spiral into depression. Putting your soul down on paper and allowing the world to take a peek into it is frightening. You are baring you innermost self to strangers; you are stripping off the protective cloak of normalcy that you have worn all these years and exposing your innermost self—leaving you cold, shaking and vulnerable. But writing is also a cathartic process, and I hope I can find release from the shadows that have stalked me all my life. I hope I can move on with a clean slate, my heart, mind and soul cleansed of the filth that has coated them.

But somewhere deep down within me, I wonder. Is it really possible? Will I ever find that much-anticipated release? Can I really wipe the slate clean and move on unburdened and free? Totally cleansed and without the burdensome baggage. Can I ever sleep peacefully night after night, without waking up to nightmares and revolting memories? Can I ever put a plug on the fear that still lurks like a cat in the darkness? I don't know. I honestly don't know. All I know and all I want is closure. I must find closure to live the rest of my life without the weight and burden of my past. And if the process of writing about my life and exposing its darkest nooks and corners to the light is what is required… I am willing to do so. I need closure like a thirsty man in the desert yearns for water. It will help my parched soul to become whole again, filled with love and light instead of hate and blackness.

I shake off my gloomy thoughts and look around me. I've come for a short break to an alpine city and the beauty of my surroundings lifts my heart. As I sit outdoors sipping a hot cup of soup in the nippy air, I soak in the splendour of the snow-capped peaks of the Alps, gazing in wonder at the famous 'golden terrace' My son and my partner—the two loves of my life—are away on the ski slopes so I am alone in this mountain paradise.

I do not ski; I did try but I don't like slippery slopes. I can't even ride a bicycle, something I should have learnt in my childhood. Without a father or a brother around, there was no one to teach me. The trust we placed on the first male member who was close to our family was misplaced. He turned out to be a demon, a self-obsessed man without a conscience or regard for anyone but to feed his greed for flesh.

When the ugliness of my memory of him flashes through my mind, it taints the exquisite environs and, God, I want to throw up my soup. I become agitated. My face pales and my hands tremble. A kind-looking couple comes up to me and asks if the seats at my table are free. They distract me from my dark thoughts, from my meanderings into my gut-wrenching past. They are like a sliver of sunshine, piercing the gloom. I smile weakly. There must be a God. But doubts cloud my mind again. If so, He should have taken away the eyes and hands of the demon before he looked at me with his lecherous eyes and touched me with his filthy, sweaty hands.

The splendour of God's creation—the majestic Alps gleaming in the buttery sunlight—touches my heart. There's so much beauty in the world. Nature is inspiring. It soothes and lifts the heart. But the world is duplicitous, double-sided. Nature can be so beautiful, so inspiring and nurturing. But it can also be cruel and unforgiving. It is like life. It comes with beauty and ugliness, with tranquillity and raging storms.

The sun may shine bright and usher in a new day every day. But deep down within me, there's so much ugliness, so much despair. I share my happy photos with my friends and muster up the courage to say I'm writing a book, yet I cannot say what it is about. I feel I need to hide my feelings. So my life looks luminous on the outside while I pour out my darkest feelings into this book with the thought that one day they will read it and know what made me feel different from them.

Until then, can I hope that my heart too will gleam clean, pure, and bright like the snow-kissed peaks? Can the sunlight penetrate its depths and cleanse it of the darkness? I can only pray. I can only hope. Maybe the cathartic process of writing will transform me, like a freshly painted landscape after a cleansing downpour.

Chapter 6
The Sanctuary and the Prison

While home was a place of despair, a place I hated and dreaded while growing up, school was a relief for me. It was an escape from that shadowy place called home. A space where I felt safe, cocooned in the knowledge that I could be myself—happy-go-lucky and happy, as every child should be. In school—my safe haven—he could not touch me. I was protected from the horrors of what happened at home.

I had always wanted to go to a school where the medium of teaching was English, unlike my sisters. I will always be grateful to Mother that she agreed to my plea. It couldn't have been easy for her to cough up the fees for a private school, but she did. Studying in an English medium school opened up a new world to me.

School laid the foundations for the person I am today, and I made some very good friends for life. In spite of the unpleasantness of my home environment, I did very well academically. I loved studying, I loved learning new things and I would absorb knowledge like a sponge. The teachers, naturally, were over the moon at having a perfect student.

My academic performance and the appreciation I received from my teachers gave me a sense of purpose and a determination to keep doing well. It also gave me a huge sense of self-worth. I felt carefree and liberated, as I could express myself in my lessons and in sports. I was also the house captain. Despite the fact that a part of me was consumed by self-hatred and shame, in school, I was a different person. I could stand up for myself. I could express myself. I was admired and looked up to. I liked being a leader. I liked being of help to fellow students who were not that bright academically. It gave me a sense of deep satisfaction to assist them in catching up with the rest of the class. Today, I seek this at work too, but it is not the same; it's a different world. I'll cover my bittersweet experiences at work in a later chapter. The fact is that I blame myself for everything that doesn't go as it should, which has taken a toll over time on both my mental and physical wellbeing.

Today, my son is going through a difficult time settling into secondary school. I almost feel guilty to tell him it was quite the opposite for me. I am, however, very content in the knowledge that he is within a safe atmosphere at home. We have a great relationship based on trust and openness and he is very comfortable speaking to me and telling me about his concerns. I try not to be overprotective, but that is easier said than done. Once a mum, always a mum! The other day, he was wandering around happily, loudly singing a song about not allowing anyone to touch inappropriately. When I think of my own past, I shudder. Can I protect my little boy? Can I ensure that he never suffers what I went through?

In this digital era, there is so much more to fear. Exposure to the internet has turned out to be a curse for so many families. There are vultures out there in the virtual world who stalk and prey on vulnerable children. And with the worldwide web being such a huge, unmonitored space, how can anyone have full control?

When I was in school, social media never existed. So we grew up free from the horrors and trauma of bullying on social media. I also believe that people were kinder then. I don't remember ever being bullied in school. It could be because I displayed leadership qualities within the environs of the school. However, in spite of all the acceptance and popularity that I gained in school, I never found a voice to express what I was going through.

Sometimes, when I reflect on the past and the present, I wonder if things would have been different if I'd had more exposure to the outside world then. By the outside world, I mean the western world, where there was and is more support for girls and for children. They are taught about *bad touch* and *good touch* at a very young age. I am not saying children in the west do not get sexually abused, but, when they do, they have the knowledge and the vocabulary to recognize that it is wrong and they also have mechanisms in place to help them, in terms of punishing the guilty, ensuring the child undergoes therapy, and law enforcement and the courts are also more amenable and understanding of the issue. The support system a child abuse victim has in the west is way superior to what a child in India could ever hope for, because they have mechanisms in place to tackle it legally with the help of a strong support system. I do believe they have more empathy too. Society does not judge the child; society instead ostracizes the perpetrator. In India, the victim is punished for the crimes of the perpetrator.

My school was run by Catholic nuns. They would give us lectures about being pure and pious. I remember one of our moral science lessons where the sister taking the class told us that we are not toys and we must not allow anyone to touch us for their pleasure. At that time, I recall how I so acutely wanted to stand up in class and tell her about the ordeal I had been facing. Yet I couldn't because I would always wonder—what if no one believes me again? This lack of confidence has not left me to date. I empathise with everyone who had the misfortune to go through the same ordeal as me. And I also salute them for not giving up and I urge them not to live in self-blame. Because the blame lies in the weak support systems and not us.

Why do victims lose their voice? Why can't they speak up? Or do these vultures choose to prey on the weak ones? I often wonder… I search my memory and prod myself to find an answer to why I couldn't scream and shout from the top of the roofs. Why couldn't I have told the teachers in school or confided in my best friends? But what would I have said? *I feel dirty. I am different from you lot. You have a father. I don't. The father figure in our home has taken advantage of the trust my family has in him. He is touching me inappropriately.* I was very disturbed and confused, another legacy I deal with even today when facing situations where I need to speak up.

Being so young and innocent there were times when I didn't even understand what was going on, what he was doing to me. I do now, and those days are best written off from my life. I retract from everyone. I need to grieve for that child to free it from within me.

So how could I have expressed the trauma I was facing? Could I have stood up in front of all my friends and confessed the sordid reality of my life at home? I was filled with shame. I was filled with fear. If my friends knew about my repugnant experiences, would they have rejected me? So many thoughts clouded my head. *Will they shun me? If their parents know, will I be invited to their home for birthday parties?* See how I detested myself and believed it was I who was at fault. So many questions flooded my little mind, leaving it awash in waves of confusion. Was I detached or in denial? Neither, I think. I was just a child who knew nothing better.

I recoil with horror when I remember how my mother had sent me with him and his friend to visit the school. I was about eight years old then. I thought he would leave me alone as his friend was there with us. But it was not to be so. I remember how, once, on the way back home, he was holding on to the handle of the car and his arm brushed against my breasts. If his friend noticed, he turned a blind eye. I was dying a thousand deaths of shame. I really longed to tell my mother about what was going on. But at that point, my childlike mind wondered whether she would understand or simply put, I didn't know how to. We were not encouraged to talk to our grownups about such things in those days unlike how it is now.

It was like wading in muddy waters and trying to make sense of things that seemed way beyond me. I felt bewildered. I wondered whether males had the right to do whatever they desired in order to satisfy their cravings. No matter if it was a child and it was without consent. This was my reality. This was what I had experienced from a tender age. So, would telling anyone change it all? Was this the natural way of life? At eight, how deeply could I think? How much did I understand? And who was there for me? After all, the monster was looked up to by the family (and, believe it or not, he still is). Was he a good man? Was I a bad girl? Was what he was doing all right? Deep down I knew it wasn't but a part of me was unsure. I floated in this murky lake, trying to stay afloat as he pulled me down.

Brushing against my breasts was just one of so many horrific incidents. There are so many more dreadful ones, but they are just too repugnant for me to touch upon. I am not ready to expose myself so totally to the world.

But when I remember all those awful, debasing incidents, I feel shivers run down my spine, my hands tremble, and I can feel the bile rising in my belly. I can smell his foul breath, remember that awful feeling of his slimy hands exploring my body—the body of a guileless child. The monster, the vulture, preying on me and taking his fill as if it was his birth right.

Naturally, I started reacting to the trauma I was facing. There was this anger that raged deep within me, and I began to express my suffering through heated outbursts. My family was baffled and had no idea what was causing me to behave in this way. I would fly into fits of rage at home and bang my head against the wall, lock myself in my room, and not eat or drink for hours. I carried that feeling of injustice with me into my adult life. My friends teased me that I was always raging and couldn't bear things not going the way they should. Incidents which were small to others were big to me, I didn't like it when they turned up late when we had agreed to a set time or if someone cancelled an event at the last minute. I took it personally. I also hated my own company, so I was always seeking the company of others. The fear of being alone goes back to my childhood experience.

All the trauma and the pressure of keeping things to myself was taking its toll on not only my mind but my body too. I was internalizing everything and that was traumatic for a young child. How heavy a burden could I bear at that tender age? I lost my appetite and would barely eat. As a result, I became very skinny and my immune system got compromised. I contracted jaundice and caught every seasonal bug, just some more things to add to the litany of woes that already threatened to subsume my life.

To make matters worse, I got my periods at a very young age. I had not been told about periods so when I found myself bleeding, I was alarmed and thought I was going to die. I thought this had happened due to him touching me there. I hid it from everyone. I wasn't spared humiliation even during my periods because the monster would try to stick his hand inside my clothes. My dignity, my everything was taken and forsaken. As teenagers, especially in those days, even something as normal as a bodily function like menstruation was something shameful, something we hid from the world. It wasn't something we talked about and we would be mortified if someone talked about our periods. And to double the shame, here was the monster pawing me even during *those* times. I could have curled up and died, such was the humiliation, shame, and helplessness that I felt.

Around this time, I started losing all confidence. I was wrapped up in a world of mortification, a secret world I couldn't speak about. I turned into an introvert and began to avoid family functions and weddings. I was painfully shy, hiding within the protective bubble I had created around myself. I hated my skinny body and the way my clothes would hang on me. I felt ugly. I felt totally out of place. I felt all alone.

It was only in school that I felt like myself. It was my escape, my sanctuary. I blossomed in school under the watchful eyes of Mother Mary. I was lucky to have had this solid foundation, both literally and physically. The foundation that was laid for me in school gave me not only knowledge but also helped me to evolve as a person. I may have been a hollow shell at home, but within the cocooned environs of my beloved alma mater, I shone. And later in life, that has stood me in good stead. My education and the inculcation of leadership qualities have helped me to become financially independent and be a success in my professional life. And helped me to gain a sense of self, however small…

But will I ever be able to forgive him? I don't think so. I want him to burn in hell, I want him to die a very slow, painful death. It would be easier, even now, if he was dead because then, I would be free—really, really free. What I mean by this is that I can visit my mother and the rest of the family without that awful fear and dread that he will show up.

Chapter 7
Home and Holidays

At home, I was like a prisoner. I had nowhere to hide, nowhere to escape to. Like a predator, he would make his moves when he was not being watched; he would seek me out even when I was asleep. When this happened, I would curse myself for being alone. My body would tense, I could feel the bile rise in my throat and a shudder run through my spine. The human mind has an amazing capacity to detach itself from the horrors it sees, hears, and experiences. And that's what my mind did. I pretended that this was not happening to me. I'd close my eyes, steel my body, and pray for the abomination to pass, to go away. At some point, while my young, delicate body was being subjected to his lechery, I would just stop feeling anything; my defenceless, innocent self would be numbed.

It was awful, just horrific to be subjected to this repeatedly, that too in my own home, by a man who the family trusted. I so desperately wanted someone to rescue me. I prayed someone would turn up and find him, shame him. But I was also suffused with humiliation and fear and would be rigid with fear that someone would see me in this state. If they had, I would have probably died of shame.

The formative years childhood are very important as they shape our later years and our entire adulthood. It's a pity that my mother never understood this. For her, doing well in school and being an obedient child were very important. She was bringing us up with only her own experience to guide her. Would it have been different if our father was still alive? I definitely believe so. I carry the fear of sleeping alone in the dark even today. And I seek the support of a father figure even now in my times of distress. I want someone to sort it out for me. I forget that I am more than capable of doing it myself. I am no longer a child, and I do not want to be a needy adult. But thanks to my scarred past, I find myself being clingy and fearful at times. It's not something I am particularly proud of.

Today, when I look back, I have so many regrets. I wonder—*what if*? What if I had not allowed myself to be degraded that way? What if I had fought back? What if I had slapped him, kicked him? My adult self looks back in dismay and wishes that I had not been so submissive, so quiet, so pliant. I wish I had shouted out, "Look, Mother! Look at what this disgusting man is doing to me. Never ever allow him to set foot in our house ever again." And I wish I could have added, "And please spare me those visits to my sister's house during the school holidays." Well, if wishes were horses, pigs would fly. Years have passed. Was I complicit in my silence? No, I don't for one moment think so. I was too young and I was a victim of patriarchy. I had taken on the heavy yoke of the burden of shame onto my frail shoulders. I simply didn't have a voice, which is a common phenomenon among victims of child sexual abuse.

You see, I was so conditioned to the society we lived in, so shaped by its mores, that I never ever thought, even once, that the shame would be upon him or that it was he who should have felt mortified. My naive mind never grasped the fact that he should be the one to be condemned. In a society so cloistered, so conservative, so dependent on appearances, I was worried that everyone would blame me. It worries me that in some households in some parts of India, and even other parts of the world, society still follows such practices. Besides my own cathartic experience of finding relief from sharing my experience, I also pray that society learns something from this. I am not just another abused child; this book is not just another tale of misery. To me, I hope it acts as an eye-opener. The consequences of not protecting or supporting a child from abusers bears a huge impact all around. It is not just the child who gets affected lifelong; it also has an effect on the relationships that the child has as a grown up too. It lurks like a dark shadow in the background, a ghost from the past that never lets you run free.

I recollect how, once, I held a blade in my hand when he came to feel me from the back. My small hand determinedly held the blade, and I made small incisions on his arm. It was a miniscule way of claiming my agency in an unfair world. And it felt good. I don't feel sorry or apologetic about my small act of rebellion, or for protecting myself. But, looking back, with the wiser eye of an adult, I realize that it was nowhere near justice. It's laughable, if it wasn't so tragic, that I thought I could stop the monster with that show of mutiny, or that I would physically deter him by cutting him with a blade.

He was not the wounded one, I was. I had scratched the surface and inflicted bodily harm on him, but it was insignificant in the larger scheme of things. My wound was so deep that it lacerated my soul. It is a wound I still carry, a wound that eats my insides like a deadly cancer. Will it ever get healed? I am told it will if I can find closure, and I am seeking that closure in all aspects through the cathartic process of writing this book. So please bear with me when I bare my soul; do not think for one moment that I am indulging in self-pity.

I remember how, after I'd cut him with the blade, the repulsive beast had the audacity to tell my sister that I had been naughty to cut him. My sister seemed indifferent. She never asked me why I had done something like that; after all, it was an act of violence by a child, and in normal circumstances should never have been condoned. In retrospect, I wonder whether she knew. Was she feeling as helpless as me? Did she feel that she too had no voice to stamp out this evil? But then, I think with an aching sadness that she was an adult and I was not. If she knew, she should have done something, anything, to protect her younger sister. I have kept quiet about this incident and my feelings about it for all these years and my mother has asked me to keep my mouth shut in order to protect my sister from the shame of not having done enough. My other sisters feel that she will not be able to bear being outed. As I write this, there is a part of me that is scared of what she will do when she reads the book. But I owe it to her son and his wife, who have stood by me and have encouraged me to go ahead.

As a reader, I need you to know that I am baring my heart and stripping my soul, exposing its tender kernel, for the world to see. I don't want to hold back anything, however gut wrenching, heart breaking, or shocking it may be. This is because I will do anything within my power to stop another child or adult from having to go through something so evil, so debasing. I will elaborate on this later in the book.

Over the years, when I began to understand the physical reactions of the body to sexual touch, I understood what he had been feeling. I know how repulsive and sickening it seems; then imagine what it would have been like for me, a child who had to go through all that emotional turmoil.

While all this turmoil was going on at home, I put on a brave face and carried on like a normal child, following my daily routine of school and studies.

School was my solace, like I said in the previous chapter. I loved my school and everything that came with it. Doing well academically and being an ideal student that any teacher could wish for—obedient, helpful, and always a top performer—brought a lot of positives into my life. It was an escape from the horrors of life at home. It was a triumph for my battered self—that I could do well in some aspect of my life, that I had control over something... that I could shine. I loved to show my report card to Mother at the end of the school year. It was my very own achievement, where I thrived in spite of my inner dark moments. I also took part in singing, drama, and sports. These were at quite a basic level, but for me, everything that distracted my mind, that helped me to forget the horrors that were my alternate reality, helped. Each little act of learning, be it academics or extracurricular activities, helped me regain confidence in myself.

I used to hate summer holidays because I was stuck at home with nothing to do. And the monster would come visiting. At least during school term, I had a place to escape to; I had homework and other activities to keep me occupied, to subdue the demons in my mind. Sometimes Mother would celebrate my birthday, which fell during the holidays, in whatever way she could afford. I would feel awkward about the simple food and that there was no fancy cake. But then, what more could a child without a father expect? Looking back, I realize that I was lucky that it was the eighties. Those were simpler times when materialism hadn't grasped us with its greedy fingers. Kids those days never compared and competed with each other on who threw the best birthday party or who had the latest iPhone or what car their parents drove. Thanks to our financial situation, I never even used to get a new birthday dress. Yet, I am grateful to my mother because she did the best she could with her limited means. For me, it was about the love and the caring.

I was a voracious reader and would read anything I could find. I used to borrow books from friends, as there was no library suitable for my age. The books I read transported me to another world, a happier world, a fantasy world that was so different from my grim reality. I dreamt of traveling one day to see the world, because there was so much out there that excited me. I am still overcome by the wonders of wanderlust and am so happy that I have the means to indulge my passion.

During my childhood, I used to also play with a friend who lived next door to us. We would play pretend school or pretend domesticity. We would dress our dolls with bits of wools and pieces of cloth we found lying around our houses. We made pretend food and set out on picnics. Those were such innocent and happy times and, in a way, were the essence of my childhood. The part of my life that was untouched, or rather sheltered, from the ongoing abuse. They were times when I could be an innocent, carefree child, playing and living in the present moment, happy to indulge in normal childhood activities with the warmth and companionship of my friend.

Looking back, I realize that I didn't do very much with my sisters. This must have been due to the age difference among us. There was always someone appearing for some exam or the other. I did visit my sisters' friends sometimes when they would take me along. Life was quite simple in those days. We played at home, visited friends and relatives, and went on the occasional outing. We were not even allowed to go to the movies unless we were accompanied by a grown up. There were no smartphones, iPads, or social media sites to occupy us.

But the worst thing about holidays was that he found it easy to drop by as I was at home all day. The beast that he was, he didn't even spare me when I was in bed with high temperature one day or, as mentioned earlier, when it was that time of the month. There were many grownups at home, including my sisters, mother, an aunt and an uncle, but none of them noticed what was happening right under their noses. The monster was brazen enough to abuse me with them being present in the house. They all looked at him as an affectionate relative, as someone who was a father figure to me. And why would they have any suspicions? After all, in a normal world, a kind world, would a father hurt his own child?

Well, life is cruel, and when I grew up, I realized that this happens everywhere, even today. Yes, fathers and even brothers sexually abuse their daughters or sisters, and, quite often, even a male child. It makes me sick, it makes me want to throw up, to scream and rant at the injustices in this world. And sadly, in India this phenomenon continues almost unchecked. In the West, awareness of child sex abuse is high and people are getting convicted. Look at the sex abuse scandal in the Catholic Church; even the dead are being called out for their sins of child sexual abuse (CSA). But in many parts of Asia and India, honour is more important, in the pecking order, than a child's trauma. The guilty are protected while the victims are left to fend for themselves—to either find justice or escape. In most cases, the family will never support them in their quest for justice. I will this to change. I need a promise from every reader (I do hope many will read it and refer it on) that they will make a difference to the life of a victim.

I often muse on the what ifs. How would my life have been if this monster had not married into the family? Would I be stronger, fearless, and free of anxiety and depression? How did I not succumb to the thoughts of taking my own life? Was I a coward for even contemplating suicide? Or am I a survivor for not succumbing to the pull of escaping by taking my own life? Well, now that I am in a better place and far away from the wretchedness of my childhood, I choose to be a survivor again and again... because through my experiences I want to help others, I want to make their voices heard. With all my heart, I want to help victims to fight the fear that engulfs others like me and everything else that comes from being a victim of CSA. I chose to live and I choose to fight and help in any which way I can. And if, through my writing, I can give a voice to the voiceless, then I will be satisfied that I have made a difference in this world and offered hope to CSA survivors who battle the blackness of their lives.

Chapter 8
Do You Ever Cope?

Time, they say, is the greatest healer. But sometimes, I wonder if time has just papered the wounds with a thin bandage that helps to anaesthetise the pain. Even today, there's this cold blanket of dread that often envelops me. But, even if time may not have healed me, it has definitely helped me to put things in some kind of perspective. Probably time and distance have helped me to accept what happened to me. Does that make it easier? Yes. Does that mean the pain and rage have gone away? No.

As I grew up, I possibly learnt how to deal with this revolting ordeal. There was one thing I persisted with in spite of the horror that was my life at home; I never gave up on the things which were under my control. For instance, I had insisted on studying in an English medium school and Mother had given into my pleadings.

Once I finished school and college, I knew that the only way I could escape from his evil clutches was to leave my home town, leave Assam. And the only way to do that was to pursue higher education. I fought tooth and nail to be sent to the city of my dreams, far away from the malevolent presence of the demon. If I needed to heal, to be able to do something with my life, I had to get away and put as much distance as possible between the monster and me. That was my only hope for salvation, the only way I could start life afresh.

As I left my childhood days behind and blossomed into adulthood, I found ways to avoid him more and more. With school behind me, I no longer had school holidays, so I was not packed off to his house during the vacations. My life was busy and I had so much to do. I had to prepare for my exams and attend tuitions so that I would obtain a good grade to get into university.

Once I joined college, I tasted the sweet nectar of freedom. I was no longer chaperoned everywhere. I was allowed to travel by myself and could even visit my friends' places. I avoided him as much as I could and snatched every opportunity I got to stay away from his evil presence.

But if I was persistent, he was even more tenacious. He just never gave up. I still remember the day he strolled into my room on the pretext of speaking to me about my future studies. The vile creature that he was, he actually propositioned me to sleep with him. He said that he had waited too long and that it was time he 'had' me. I stared at him in disbelief, feeling sick to the stomach and angry. I defiantly asked him why I should comply.

Suddenly, deep within me, I felt this surge of confidence. I was no longer that little girl who he could bend to his will. I was ready to fight back tooth and nail to preserve my existence. At that moment, I knew he realised that I could defend myself. I stood up, shaking with anger, and firmly told him to go away and never speak to me again. I reminded him that he had a wife and that his boys were growing up and that he should care about them instead. But the thick-skinned monster was unmoved; he brushed aside my anger, my concerns, my requests. Instead, he brazenly told me that I should not worry; he had the gall to say that he would book a hotel and provide me protection.

As I write about his disgusting propositioning, I am seething with rage. I know I skipped this bit in the earlier chapters because, somewhere, I couldn't bring myself to write about it; it was so humiliating, so nauseating. But penning this book is about freeing myself, about acknowledging what happened to me and, thereby, not only healing myself but helping others. So, by avoiding the worst memories, I cannot free myself. I will stay shackled in this prison of shame and humiliation. I know I will never get back those years that I wasted on negative, toxic thoughts. But by letting it all out, maybe I can soar on the wings of a new life, unshackled by the past. As a result, I decided that I need to squeeze every bit of the venom out of my system.

The bastard had had it all planned in his head. Looking back, I wonder—*how could he?* My thoughts are a jumble because there's so much that I can't make sense of. Was it because he is sick in the head? Should be receive treatment? Should he be punished by the law, or both?

I kept all this hidden within me for so many long years, buried deep in my heart and head. But the world has now caught up with me. Now that I have been exposed to the ugly underbelly of humankind, realization dawned on me that I am not the only one who has had to suffer these indignities which strip you of your very essence. There are so many reports of abuse, and so many men and women are coming out and sharing their stories in order to be heard and to claim justice for what they had to endure. I too dare to dream—that one day I will get my justice, my answers, and my revenge even. There's something comforting about dreaming about all the possible scenarios.

But then, reality gives me a good shake and I snap out of my reverie. Will I ever get my justice? The sad truth is most likely not... As a reader, you are possibly wondering why. Well, it's complicated. The society I grew up in is conservative and there are so many other factors that come into play as well. We all know that life is not black and white; it has so many shades of grey in between. It's not like a Hollywood film where the good guys go blazing in with guns to eliminate or lock up the bad guys. If only life had such simple endings—where good always triumphed over evil.

So let me try and explain the many reasons why I cannot expose him or name and shame him. I grew up with his family and spent many holidays there. So, while I detest the monster and couldn't care less about him, his wife and boys have been good to me. His wife is a typical product of a patriarchal community and firmly believes that he is a good husband and a good father to her boys.

Of course, there are times when I wonder whether she knew. Was she an enabler? Had she been turning a blind eye all along? Is she letting us all down by being selfish because she wants her husband to be seen as a good man? Has she kept silent and turned the other way to keep up a façade in society to protect the family's reputation?

I am very close to his elder son. After he got married and when he was expecting his first child, I went insane with worry. So many thoughts crowded into my head, causing my anxiety levels to spike. I had sleepless nights because my mind was filled with questions, doubts, fears. My biggest fear was this: *What if he gets his filthy, lecherous hands on the child to come?* Finally, I discussed my fears with my therapist, and together we decided that I needed to tell him (the son). It was a difficult decision and even more difficult to put into action. But my conscience would not allow me to remain silent, because then I could be complicit in future abuse. With great difficulty, I mustered up all my courage and talked to his son's wife; it was my attempt to protect the monster's grandchildren from him. The wife was shocked; no one can swallow such a bitter dose of ugly truth with equanimity. But she was relieved and grateful that I had shared the truth with her. However, she didn't want to expose the monster or have the truth come out within their close circles because she felt that it would hurt the family and their close relatives. That is the Indian mentality—keep all the skeletons rattling in the cupboard and present a smokescreen of normality. After all, it's reputation that matters—the gloss on the surface. The ugliness inside can be concealed. Anyway, I did what I could and I thank her for her support.

Once a molester, always a molester. That is what I believe and that is why I decided to tell the son's wife. If there is hell, my molester is a prime candidate to rot there. In my eyes, especially after what I suffered under his sway as a young child, he doesn't deserve the loyalty of his family. His wife is what one can call a drama queen, always making a mountain out of a molehill. She is the type to create scenes when things don't go her way. My mother is intimidated by her and warned me to me to keep the ugly truth away from her. My mother believed that she would either blame me or create a further scandal by attempting suicide.

This is the sordid reality of a patriarchal society, a conservative society with a herd mentality, where all that matters is appearances. The honour of the family. Instead of supporting me in my attempt to reveal the sleazy truth about him, everyone, including my sisters, agreed that it should be buried. Imagine the shame and the loss of honour if my sisters' in-laws and their relatives got to know that the youngest sister was not 'pure', that she had been sullied, that she was 'damaged goods'. Our family's reputation would have been in tatters. If it wasn't so tragic, it would have been funny. Isn't it ironic? I was the one who had been molested for years by that beast, but if the truth came out, my family and I would be the ones to suffer disgrace.

So, if you ever think that I have gained something by not revealing him, it is quite the contrary. Over the years, there have been so many times when I stopped talking to my mother and sisters. Their hypocrisy and their lack of support hurt me, angered me, disgusted me. Sometimes, the agony of facing this all alone, in silence, would make me feel as if someone had stabbed me in the stomach. I would double over in pain, clutching my stomach and rolling into a foetal position, to protect myself from the harsh realities of a cruel world.

In order to protect my family and their reputation and standing in society, I kept silent. I didn't want them to have to face the consequences of my outing the beast. Instead, I suffered in silence. And that evil bastard used that to his full advantage. He knew he could get away with his beastly acts because the people around me would not protest or take action against him. They were, instead, complicit with their silence.

This book is my chance to expose him and, even though I feel I should still protect his wife, I no longer really care. Too much has happened. By staying silent all these years and bottling up my emotions, it is only I who have been affected. All the rest continue to go about their lives normally, pretending that all is well. After all, my sisters were not the ones abused; I was. I was the one who suffered and it is I who is still coming to terms with the trauma and shame. Through this cathartic but traumatic writing process, I expose myself to the world, like a snail without a shell.

To make matters worse, I must tell you this too. He is a politician belonging to one of India's top parties; he was even a member of parliament—one of the most powerful posts in India. In India, rapists, murderers and thieves get elected to parliament with alarming regularity, so I am not surprised that he became a member of the 'hallowed house'. This is the sorry state of affairs in my country—a molester, a selfish, avaricious fiend is held in a high position of power. People look up to him with respect and genuflect in his presence, as if he is some god. With all his sycophantic minions flocking around him and the kind of power he holds, he is smug in the knowledge that he can do anything and get away with it. With some misplaced hope for justice, I even wrote to the leader of his political party, and, guess what, I never even received an acknowledgement. In India's political system, no one cares about the morality of a politician; all they care about is whether he or she can bring in votes or money. Morals be damned.

I cringe when the family, including Mother, takes his name with respect even today. You know what? I have come to the conclusion that even though they know what has happened, they pretend not to know. They prefer to live in denial and bury their heads under the sand like an ostrich. It's so much easier that way. Over time, my sisters have acknowledged the abuse I went through and seem to have understood it to a certain degree. They had watched this television series hosted by a famous Indian actor, where he spoke to victims of sexual abuse. That was an eye opener for them and they said that they finally understood the ordeal that I had gone through. They were so blinded by the foolish notions of patriarchy and honour fed to them within the cocoon of a small city and closed society that it took a television programme for them to realise the pain and damage that I had endured.

Through the years, I felt so alone, so cut off from my near and dear ones. What helped me was to mentally run through my sessions with my therapist. I realised that the only person who can help me is myself, I am now an adult and I can speak to the child I was back then, to nurture and protect her. This was the best advice I got from my therapist. Today, whenever I feel anxious or disturbed, I pretend that I am sitting down next to my five-year-old self and I comfort her with soothing and calming words. It was a very difficult, heart-wrenching session, when I had to meet my child self with the help of my therapist. I kept avoiding it because I felt I had failed her. And when I succeeded in finally connecting with my childhood self, I broke down and the tears poured down my face like a deluge. I sigh heavily as I look back at that day; it was a cathartic but harrowing experience. It remains fresh in my mind as if it was yesterday.

Can I be blamed for losing faith and trust in relationships and people in general, even in myself? After what I've gone through, where even my family was not there to help me, I guess not. I had no one to turn to; I had only myself to depend upon and later my therapist, who guided me and helped me to get out of the cycle of self-loathing and self-doubt. But even today, I feel I always have to be on guard and fight my way through life, possibly like so many other women across the globe. I cannot stand injustice. I always stick up for myself and for others. Some may see this as being hot-headed. But you know what, I'm past caring. The world is still an unjust place for women, and unless we fight back, we will continue to suffer the onslaught of patriarchy and an unjust world. Beastly men, like the monster, can dehumanize us but they cannot take away our essence. We cannot allow them to keep us in bondage forever.

Chapter 9
A Ray of Hope

When you suffer sexual abuse for so long, it is but natural to start loathing yourself. There was a time when I hated everything about myself. I felt like a misfit everywhere I went. Even today, in spite of all the therapy I've been through and my own self-healing process, there are times when I still feel that self-hatred threatening to overcome me; there are still moments when I feel I don't fit in anywhere. Despite everything, I plodded on, the burden of low self-esteem notwithstanding. Even though I felt this deep sense of helplessness and was weighed down by it, I tried to never let it show.

Today, I may be a successful woman with a happy life, which includes a devoted partner and a beautiful son, but I still feel vulnerable and often have this feeling that something bad will happen to me. To an onlooker, I am a beautiful, intelligent, and strong woman. Little do they know how fragile I feel. That feeling of insecurity hovers around me; it settles like a fog very often, only to lift and give me a clearer, happier vision of the world. It suddenly dawns on me that I always tend to look for someone to protect me, look after me, and sort things out for me. Actually, the reality is that all along, I have done it all for myself. My lack of confidence does not allow me to give myself credit for what and who I am today. I guess my sense of self is fractured.

Another useful affirmation that my therapist told me to practise was to write down a list of all the positive aspects of my personality that my friends praise me for. She advised me to keep this list somewhere where I can see it often in order to reaffirm myself. She also told me to always pat myself on my back (literally) for any positive achievement, however small it may seem to me.

There are so many times when I sit there and just wish... I wish I could erase all those awful times... I wish I could erase all those dark memories... I wish I could blot out the past and start life afresh so I can feel totally free, like a carefree bird soaring in the sky, and enjoy life with my precious son. Then I become philosophical and I wonder, would that also make a better person of me? Someone once told me that God gives the hardest challenges to the strongest as He knows who can come out a winner at the other end. Can I claim to be one of those He chose? My friends swear by this. I'll leave that for you to decide. Before that, I have some more experiences to share with you so that you have a clearer picture of what my life has been like.

However brave I may seem to the world around me, I have to admit that there were many times when I just felt like giving up—I wished I could catch a terminal disease and just die a most welcome death. And yes, the sweet but dark temptation to end it all did haunt my thoughts occasionally. I remember how I once managed to get some rat poison, but, thankfully, I could not get myself to take that final step. I guess I always was a fighter even if I had to swim desperately against the strong currents that battered me; somehow I stayed afloat and kept my head above water. Because giving up would mean letting the vultures and the so-called keepers of society win. Something in me kept giving me the power to fight. I firmly believe that my faith in God made me persevere, made me strong. I am a great believer in the Almighty. While growing up, my mother was my role model. I never saw Mother give up when Father died, in spite of all the hardships she faced while bringing us up. I have this huge admiration for her because what she did was not easy, that too in a closed, traditionalist society like ours and with all the financial problems she had to face as well. But I also have an equal amount of anger and hurt towards her for letting me down. Yes, I know, it's complicated. But that is how I feel. A strange amalgam of admiration and misgivings. My mind is a quagmire.

When all the abuse was happening, I prayed to God; in fact, so desperate and heartbroken was I that I prayed to the gods of all religions. My trusting mind kept believing that things would get better. I would keep telling myself: *One more day; just bear it for one more day. Face it and don't think about ending your life. Something better has to happen.* This faith, this hope… kept me from ending it all. Or, if you believe in kismet or destiny, well, I guess that my time hadn't come. I had to go through my role, my part. I was playing on the stage of life and I had to enact my role. The show must go on!

A spiritual leader once told me that what we go through is a bodily experience on this stage; our souls are the real beings and our souls do not get tainted. Her words struck a chord with me immediately; I just felt so deeply that these words of wisdom applied to me, and that gave me strength and some kind of reassurance.

Let me tell you a secret—deep, deep down within me, I know I have that indefinable something that will help me to pull myself up no matter what. I have these hidden reserves of strength. You will understand what I mean by this as you read on and you will comprehend why I say this with such conviction. In fact, I believe, no, I *know*, that each one of us is special and each one of us has a gift; all we need to do is identify our gift. Sometimes, we may need the help of a friend, a therapist, or a spiritual leader to reveal it to us. But I have a deep conviction that whatever life may throw at us, it is definitely worth living.

Consequently, with the maturity and the wisdom that I gained over the years, I came to a realisation—a powerful one—that not loving oneself is not an option. We have been dealt with a hand of cards in this drama of life; we need to play that hand. Some say its karma, some don't believe in karma. Whatever you believe in, make it work for you. If you do not value yourself, why should others? I keep telling my son this. I once told him that if he calls himself stupid, it means he has insulted his genes. The poor kid took it literally and apologised to me profusely.

I had a demon in my life who stole my childhood. And the effects of his evil actions continue to trouble me in my adulthood. But I've realised that I am *not* a victim. Just because some monster has taken away a part of who we are, or if life has been unfair to us, it doesn't mean everyone is against us. Even if no one is on your side, you have the power within you to look after yourself. You need to think positive. Before the negative thoughts take over and submerge you, seek help. There's nothing wrong or weak in seeking help. And if you don't want to do that, but would rather try something else, that is fine too. We are not cut from the same cloth. We come from different backgrounds, countries, ethnicities, and cultures. So do whatever works for you. But *do something*, because if you don't, the demons will win. We are not weak; we are strong because each one of us is a survivor. Develop your inner strength and look ahead with the knowledge that nothing lasts forever. In life, there is always a reason to hope because we don't know what the future will bring. But as long as we are alive, there is always a likelihood that life will shower us with good things and happiness. Trust in the universe, in the goodness of people, in God.

While writing this book, I have read about so many other survivors and, in the process, I have learnt a lot from their experiences. I've felt their pain and I've cried when I've heard their stories. I thank them for sharing their pain and their learnings with the world. Since I am in the process of opening myself up to the world and exposing my deepest secrets, I know how hard it must have been for them. But, yes, after all that I've been through and, thanks to my therapy and the love that I bask in from my son and my partner, the black cloud that surrounded me may not have disappeared entirely, but rays of sunlight have broken through the gloom, heralding a dawn of hope and healing.

Chapter 10
Not Conventional...

Once I left the safe cocoon of school, I got admission in the best college in my town. It was a complete change from the cocooned environment of school and quite a culture shock for someone like me who came from such a sheltered background. The college was a co-educational institute, so I was interacting freely with members of the opposite sex for the first time. The sudden freedom to mix with boys was quite heady for many of my friends, who started going on clandestine dates. Why clandestine? Because it was frowned upon for boys and girls to go out together alone. In an old-fashioned, rigid society like ours, especially in those days when arranged marriages were the norm, it was considered wrong to date or have a boyfriend or girlfriend. Ironically, the innocent act of dating, or mingling with the opposite sex, was not causing any harm to anyone. But in a traditional society where people had closed minds, it was an issue. They wanted to repress youngsters and not allow them to enjoy what is natural—to hang out with people of the opposite sex, or even be attracted to them.

I had a large group of friends, but I didn't have a boyfriend. I didn't consider myself pretty enough to be asked out. I guess all the trauma had battered my sense of self-worth. Also, hailing from a conservative and almost deprived upbringing, I dressed very modestly compared to my peers. I couldn't afford to splurge on the latest fashions. I had to save up every penny so that I could hang out in the canteen with my friends or go out once in a while to a restaurant. The sisters who were just a little older than me and I shared our outfits so we could have some variety in our wardrobe. In that aspect, school had been so much easier because we all had to wear uniforms, which was a great leveller. So, even though I came from a marginalised background, it was not as evident as it was in college. I could wash and re-wear my uniform over and over again and I only needed two pairs of shoes.

Sometimes, I would visit the main market in town with my sisters or my friends. There were no swanky shopping malls in those days. We would troop around the crowded market and hunt for clothes and stuff at bargain pieces; if we got fabric, we would take it to the family tailor and haggle with him to stitch the clothes for us at lower rates. There was no concept of student discounts, so students hailing from underprivileged families and the not-so-poor working class paid the same prices.

At college, the lessons were dull but I enjoyed the company of my friends. I met someone new from my neighbourhood and we became very good friends. She and I used to travel to college together, sharing the rickshaw fare, which was a big bonus for me since I was into saving every penny I could. We would also travel together for the tuitions we needed to take to catch up on lessons that some of the teachers didn't cover well in class. Often, the teachers would do this so that they could make an extra buck by offering tuition.

I was heartbroken when I found out, after a few years, that my friend had passed away during childbirth. By then, I had moved out of India and had lost touch with her. This was before the age of social media, way before friends could be reunited on Facebook. During my time in college with her, there were so many moments I had wanted to talk to her and unburden myself. I did try, but I just couldn't bring myself to do so. I was worried that I would cause her pain by confessing the truth of my sordid past to her. And now, I'm so glad that I didn't as she left this world without the burden of my dark truth. I still dream of her sometimes, especially on days when I'm feeling blue. Thinking of her is a source of solace for me. It takes me back to happier days, to our carefree days of college and youth. It's as if she comes to me to comfort me, calling out to me to saying, "Come on, get up, we've got to," just like she used to when she would come to pick me up to head to college, and I would be lying in bed ill or depleted.

My college fees, transportation, and tuition fees drained my mother's already meagre resources, and I felt really terrible for her and also guilty. I made up my mind that one day I would look after her as a payback for all the sacrifices she was making.

When I was in school, I had the luxury of travelling in a private school bus, so I was sheltered from the rogues who inhabit public transport like parasites. But during my college days, there were times when I would have to travel by public transport. I can still vividly remember one particular incident. A man who was standing next to me started to lean on me, and soon had his groin pressed into my back. It was such a yucky feeling and I was disgusted. I immediately whirled around and sharply told him to move away. However, he didn't, so I gave him a hard slap across his face. The ladies on the bus started applauding me and the bus conductor threw the pervert out of the bus.

I wish that it was that simple to deal with abusers. Look at my reality—my main tormentor was a close family member and it was his voice that was heard and believed over everyone else's. In a public forum, I could shame a stranger and be applauded and have action taken against him. But ironically, in my own home, which should have been my haven, it was I instead who was shamed while the pervert was praised and looked up to.

The two years of college passed by in the blink of an eye. I desperately wanted to go to a big city to study further. Some of my schoolmates had already left for bigger cities and seemed to be having a great time there. But Mother had many reasons for not sending me. The first reason was, of course, that money was tight. But she also worried about my safety. She thought big cities were dangerous. Isn't it bizarre? I was not in the least bit safe at home because I had been at the mercy of my tormentor from childhood and my mother had never kept me safe, and here she was, concerned about my safety outside the house and the town that I lived in.

It took me a year and a lot of angry outbursts to finally get my way. And suddenly, I had wings! I left my claustrophobic home town for the big city of my dreams. I had chosen to study microbiology in college and my grades were consistently good. While Mother was happy that I was doing well, she would have been much happier had I studied medicine or engineering, which were considered prestigious courses to pursue. This was and is so typical of Asian parents. Studying to get an honours degree in microbiology is a compromise, because what one should aim for is to become a doctor or engineer. I hope I do not become like my mother when my son reaches the age when he will choose what he wants to pursue in terms of his education. As far as I am concerned, he is free to pursue whatever he wants. I am so happy to see him enjoy his music; he has a great talent for it whereas I consider myself tone deaf.

I enjoyed my time at university even though it was not as eventful for me as it was for some of my peers.

Even at university, I concentrated on my studies and had a limited social life. I had no boyfriends then either, simply because I was not sought after. But, looking back, I realise that I was suffering from a massive inferiority complex. It was not just the trauma of my childhood but also the culture shock. Here I was, a small-town girl, suddenly thrust into the hustle-bustle of city life. And to this day, I feel different from the others, something only I know of and feel. I realise that it would be unfair to expect anyone else to fully comprehend my feelings.

I relished all that the big city had to offer. It was like this magical place with so much going on; things I hadn't seen in my conservative home town. There were so many things that were new to me. It was thrilling to go to multiplex cinemas that were screening the latest Hollywood movies or to shake a leg at a disco.

There was this marvellous sense of freedom; after all I was away from his evil clutches. However, I missed home; after my sheltered upbringing and growing up in a large family, I was suddenly overcome with an aching sense of loneliness.

There was this heavy burden of melancholy that I carried with me. I felt alone, isolated. Looking at all the fashionable, sophisticated people around me, I felt inadequate. I thought that I was different from the others. It was really a catch-22 situation. The positives were escape from the monster and freedom in a new city, the excitement of college life, and making new friends. But the negatives were homesickness and loneliness, and also a niggling sense of not belonging.

Guwahati in those days was a quiet, verdant town, so the shock of being in a polluted, crowded, chaotic city was a bit too much to bear initially. I longed for the greenery, the trees, the view of the mist-shrouded hills, and the glistening Brahmaputra as it snaked its way across the plains. Instead all I saw around me was bedlam. The air was smoggy, everything was dusty, and it was so noisy too.

I craved for the ordinary while being in the midst of the extraordinary. There I was in a vibrant metro city—a place that I had chosen to be in— that had so much to offer, but I still felt inadequate, I felt like a misfit and was socially awkward too. I felt I had pretend to like everyone and join them in the small chit-chats that would take place late into the night or mingle at student get-togethers. I was constantly wearing this mask and pretending to be someone I wasn't. In retrospect, I realise that it was probably due to self-esteem issues. You see, when you lose the core of your being, it leaves a mark in every aspect of your life. It's like cold ice freezing your heart. Whenever I thought of my dirty secret, this well of hatred would rise in me, and I would hate my home, my mother, and the monster. But I had to keep shut and bury all the ugliness under a cheerful, friendly mask. Why did I do that? Why did I live that life of pretence? Why did I try so hard to please everyone? Was I weak or was I a martyr? I'll never know. Maybe, deep down, I wanted to be loyal to my mother? I don't know...

Feeling different from the other girls was not a good space to be in; it took me to dark places and even darker moods. I would feel lonely in a room full of people; I was seeking something to fill the emptiness within me. With the benefit of hindsight, I realise that I was looking for love. I wanted to belong, to feel the cosy warmth of being secure. I considered myself deficient in all aspects be it my looks or my financial capabilities or charisma—you name it and I felt I lacked it. I started believing that what had been dealt to me by fate was all my fault. I was born to be wretched. Did someone not say that I had brought bad luck to my family? That with my birth came the death of my father. I was ill-fated, and I cursed myself for all the adversities that I had faced in life. I wish someone had told me then—like the therapists and healthcare professionals have now—that nothing was my fault. I was a victim of circumstances beyond my control. And most importantly for me now, I am the lucky recipient of love and admiration from my partner, who never even once would allow me to believe that I am deficit in any way.

Over time, once I got used to the rhythm of big city life and formed a few meaningful friendships, the loneliness began to ease. Life in a fast-paced metropolis barely gives you time to think. As my confidence grew and I started to become more comfortable with my new life, I started receiving a reasonable amount of interest from boys, but I didn't fancy anyone. There was one boy who pursued me persistently so finally, I went on a date with him. When he tried to hold my hand, I froze. I wanted to run away because I felt impure and confused. The only man who had touched me till then had been the evil monster, and so I associated touch from the opposite sex as something that was tainted. He stole everything from me and deprived me of the pleasure I should have got from normal experiences.

Anyway, I was getting by, and my life went on, punctuated by college, friends, studies, and outings. As college life drew to a close, I didn't know what I would do after university; however, most of my peers did. They had plans to go abroad for studies. Some had already met their life partners and were starting to plan their weddings. I wanted to travel and study abroad but I was worried about squeezing Mother's already limited finances any further. I had to find a way to continue my education. I was very worried because if I didn't forge a path for my future, I would be called back home, and that could not happen. It could *never* happen…

Chapter 11
Once Bitten, Twice Shy

Most spiritual leaders always say that you attract what you think. Well, in my case, since I'd experienced so much of darkness in my life, my thought process was always melancholy—this maelstrom of toxic, black clouds that swirled within me, shutting out the warmth of optimism and all the simple joys that life offers. And that spiralled into a vicious cycle of further darkness and sadness. I guess I had this knack for attracting negativity into my life, inviting it into my presence even though it was an unwelcome guest. It seemed as if it was branded into my DNA— to get the worst possible deal, the worst possible hand of cards that life had to deal.

And that was how life in university played out for me. It appeared to stack one disaster after another in my already fragile ecosystem. My default state was one of negativity. I woke up with this fog of blackness enveloping me in its deathly hold.

Just to give you an example: I contracted malaria. I mean, what were the chances of contracting malaria in Mumbai, when I never did so growing up in a malaria-susceptible region? The irony of it all! And, to make matters worse, I ended up contracting a serious bout of the disease, so severe that I was incapacitated. I was ill for a year and had a relapse as well. Consequently, I ended up losing an academic year.

I was wracked with guilt for letting Mother down. Despite her precarious financial situation and her misgivings, she had sacrificed so much to send her daughter to the big city. And she had invested so much hope in me.

I lost a year due to the illness. It was a terrible time—I was all alone, cut off from my family and loved ones, far away from the place I called home. I was an anonymous stranger in this teeming, chaotic city—insignificant in the larger scheme of things. I was in a dark place, a very dark place.

Feelings of inadequacy overwhelmed me. My friends had moved ahead and I was stuck. I was helpless. I was ill—my body and soul battered by fatigue, fever, and a sense of failure. Being sick is bad enough, but being sick in a strange place, far from everything familiar is even worse. It makes you feel so alone, so totally alone and bereft. Like a ship-wrecked sailor marooned on a remote island.

I missed my friends, especially my roommate. We had become very close and used to be referred to as the inseparable twins. All my life, I had yearned for appreciation and acceptance, more so at university. And now, with this illness hollowing me out, I needed it even more. My confidence had been shaken and was at its lowest ebb.

One evening, when I was hanging out with my gang of friends, I got close to a boy. He stared showing an interest in me and I got led by him. He started by paying me compliments, then holding my hand, and eventually kissing me; I didn't object as I never felt that it was wrong. I was feeling alone and adrift, and just needed love, support, admiration. However, my close friends didn't approve of my behaviour. They believed that my innocent flirtation had gone beyond kissing and refused to believe me when I told them that nothing more had happened. They started treating me like a pariah, with complete disdain. I remember how utterly lonely I felt the first time I had breakfast on my own. It was heart-wrenching for me. At that age, we need friends, we need the warmth of companionship. It defines so many aspects of our life—that heady feeling of being part of a gang, of giggling, chatting, and enjoying the camaraderie of friendship. Instead, they just cut me off—set me adrift in a sea of loneliness.

I was fraught with desolation and isolation. All alone in this mammoth city, trying to deal with my illness and all the demons inside me. I couldn't bear the extra burden of being ostracised. I thought, if I opened up to them and confided in them about my dark past, they would understand me, comprehend my motivations, be compassionate, and welcome me back into the warm fold of friendship. Yes, I guess I was clutching at straws but I dreaded not being part of the gang. I needed the security blanket of my friends; I needed to be a part of something bigger than myself; I needed people to understand and accept me. I couldn't bear the cold reality of loneliness, of being out of favour, of having no one to hang out with.

So, I opened up and bared my fragile soul to them. I told them how I still carried the scars of the abuse I had faced from childhood to adulthood. However, if I had expected compassion, understanding, or acceptance, I was sadly mistaken. They couldn't comprehend what I was saying or, maybe, they didn't know how to. Perhaps, it was something beyond what they had experienced or known in their sheltered lives—an evil too monstrous to wrap their heads around. Instead, they rejected me. They turned my truth against me and told me that I was indulging in self-pity. *Self-pity?* Did they even understand what I had gone through? Did they even know what it was like to have your entire childhood snatched away from you? To have been pawed and felt up by a lecherous man old enough to be your father? To have lost your innocence. To realise that your reality was one that was shrouded by evil and lust.

Their rejection was like a tipping point in my already tenuous world. It pushed me over the edge, and I found myself sinking to the bottom. I was overwhelmed with self-loathing, despair, and a sense of utter hopelessness. I felt I was to be blamed for everything after all. My sense of self-worth—whatever little there was—plummeted, and I lost faith in myself.

I didn't want to live any more. What did I have to live for? I had no friends. My family was so far away and had never supported me on this issue, ever. If no one was able to understand me, understand the deep trauma I had gone through, and be empathetic and understanding towards me, what was there for me? I needed love, I needed friendship, I needed the sanctuary of having someone look out for me, commiserate with me, lend me a helping hand, share my good times and bad. But I had no one.

I was alone—to fight the demons of my past and to face my uncertain future. Was this the life I had envisioned for myself? No. I had thought that escaping from Guwahati would help me to shake off the despondency of the past. I had imagined a carefree college life, surrounded by friends, where I could immerse myself in academia and also have fun exploring a new world and forging new friendships. But all that had come crashing down like an unstable house of cards. And now, the cards that life had dealt me seemed like those of a loser.

I wanted to end it all. I'd had enough. If the clouds on the choppy horizon had no silver lining, if they were murky and offered no promise of hope, then what did I have to look forward to?

I took an overdose of painkillers. Well, even that turned out to be a failure. The worst it did was to make me very sleepy. A friend's boyfriend took me to my local guardian's house, who was a distant relation.

Today, when I look back on that botched suicide attempt and its aftermath, I realise that my local guardian was one of the best women I have ever known. She didn't judge me or reprimand me. Instead, she accepted me into her home without judging me, without bombarding me with questions. In her home, I found the peace and acceptance I had craved for so long.

Losing a year is no big deal; you realise this in retrospect. But at that time, as a young, naïve student, it affected me greatly. And she understood this. She gave me space to heal, to come to terms with life, while she comforted me with her presence, her empathy, her nurturing, and her acceptance. She rallied around me and gently got me to stand on my own two feet again. She helped me see the good within me; she drilled it into me that a failure is not final. I still remember her inspiring words: *Without failure you will not be able to taste the sweetness of success.* She was always kind to me and even complimented me on my figure. She reminded me that as much as we expect friends to be kind and selfless, in reality this did not always happen.

It's funny, isn't it? There I was believing that my friends would stand by me. Instead they had deserted me like rats fleeing a sinking ship. And this lady, who I had barely known till then, had welcomed me with tenderness and love, accepted me with no questions asked, and helped me to heal and believe in myself.

Sometimes in life, it is the most unexpected people who help you. To date, she stills adores me and believes that I am an extremely talented woman. Thanks to her, I started to believe that there are good people in the world.

When I look back on that dark period in my life today, I forgive those friends. As an adult, and after having undergone therapy and experienced the healing touch of spirituality, I am able to understand that they were ignorant, they were blind. They could only see what lay in front of them and were morally flawed.

After my failed suicide attempt, I had no friends. Even my roommate, who I had thought was my soul sister, my twin, had cold-shouldered me. One of the 'friends' even went to the extent of asking her father—who knew the monster—to let the family know that I had gone off the rails. She had created the perfect circumstances for him to influence my mother to persuade me to return home.

I understand that for most people, especially those who have never suffered CSA, it is difficult to comprehend something so horrific. It can sound unbelievable to most. And for others, who don't want to think that the world could be such an evil place, the only mechanism to protect oneself from the possibility of such depravity is to shut it out, to deny the probability of something so monstrous happening in real life.

My friends needed something to open their eyes to the sordid reality of child sex abuse, which plays out across the globe. And later, their eyes were opened once the media started covering the despicable truth of CSA. Or this is what I believe. I got in touch with them much later in life, seeking to clear the air. They told me that they had judged me based on their background, education, and upbringing. India, being deeply conservative, my behaviour was judged through the unforgiving lens of patriarchy and rigid conservativeness. But then I wonder... maybe they were fair-weather friends. I don't want to judge them, I want to be different from the 'ordinary' because I was not 'ordinary'. I never judged them when they went out with their boyfriends; I wasn't even interested in knowing what they did, but I did care about them and always had their well-being in mind; I never wanted them to be hurt or harmed in anyway. Today, as I reminisce on that chapter of my life, I realise that it is their loss, because they failed to see the inherent goodness in me and also rejected the love I had for them. They lost a true friend.

So, for me, it was too late. Their platitudes and their apologies were meaningless. At a time when I was at my most vulnerable—alone and unwell—I had needed their kindness and support, but I never got it. It had taken me a lot of courage to open up to them, and their rejection of my reality, my feelings, and what had happened to me, felt like a betrayal. Thanks to them, I lost my voice and myself again. I felt judged. They had carelessly laughed at me and had looked at me with subtle contempt, as if I was a weakling not a survivor.

They had always called me the 'silly one', and the ingenuous person that I had been, I'd thought it was a term of endearment. But once the whole sordid saga played out, I recognised that this was how they had always looked at me. As the 'silly one'. I also felt that they looked down on me because my mother was not cool and fashionable like theirs, and I wasn't well off like them. But the beauty of it is that I am now living the life I want on my own terms thanks to my hard work and perseverance. I am not living off my parents or a husband. I am independent, free, and successful. I can relate this to the truth; I am living proof of what my spiritual leader would guide me about.

Well, who said life was fair? I feel a sense of liberty as I recognise that I was far ahead of them, far more mature than them. I was a survivor. I had survived the death of my father. I had survived near poverty. I had survived abuse. I had survived the denial of my family. I had fought to achieve my dreams and had come to Mumbai, leaving the cocooned existence of my childhood to embark on a new life. A small-town girl trying to chase her dreams in the city that never slept. I was brave. I was no coward. Life hadn't thrown me lemons to make lemonade; life had thrown evil at me, but I had escaped it. I wasn't unscathed by that evil; it still throws its noxious shadows on me. But, little by little, I was shaking of the malignancy and reclaiming my space, my agency.

We come alone and we go alone—don't we? So why bother if you have someone by your side or not? God or the super-being—whatever you would like to call it—has given us the strength, the power to face whatever life throws at us. My spiritual leader's words always ring in my mind: "Remember, you are a brave, powerful, peaceful, and happy soul." Which means that there is nothing we cannot overcome. Her elderly mother, who was a leading light in her times, used to tell me, "Be strong; do not let anything shake you." She passed away peacefully, not long after that. I consider myself blessed to have met her.

My stay at my local guardian's place was just what I needed. It was a space where I could lick my wounds in peace and heal with her guidance and support. I fathomed that I didn't need friends like these—so-called friends who were so shallow, so insincere, so judgemental, and so quick to abandon me at a time when I needed them the most. I didn't need heartless people like them.

When I re-joined university, I made a new set of friends who were nothing like the ones I had lost. They were true friends who accepted me for who I was without judging me or shaming me. I got my mojo back; life on campus was once again enjoyable, something to look forward to because I was no longer alone, no longer in limbo. I was enfolded in the sanctuary of friendship, of acceptance.

I started to flourish among my new set of friends. They were fun to be with and also hardworking. We would party but also burn the midnight oil when needed. But this time, I decided to keep my dirty little secret buried. I never opened up to them about my past. Once bitten twice shy, right? Or, maybe, I wanted them to know me as a happy girl, not as someone who had skeletons in her cupboard. I didn't want them to look at me as someone tainted, someone to be pitied.

Thanks to my hard work, I got my honours degree. I was a graduate! However, I didn't feel very grown up. The inner child in me still needed looking after. I didn't understand it then. I used to think I felt that way because I'd never had a father to guide me. Later on, during therapy, I was taught how to reassure the inner child within me, how to nurture her and calm her, how to help her let go of her fears. As I mentioned earlier, I have always feared being alone and even now, I am not happy in my own company. This is because I am not my best friend; I am my worst enemy. I am still learning and growing and, hopefully, one day, all the dark parts will be exorcised totally, and I will come to love myself wholeheartedly and never fear loneliness again.

My degree was a turning point in my life. So what was in store for me next?

I always tell my son that in this world, you will come across both good and not-so-good people. No one is bad by choice; in most cases, they are just ignorant. I believe we need to rise above them and keep our own counsel. He doesn't quite see this now; he is too young to grasp the complexity of it all. But I know that one day, he will remember my words and smile to himself thinking, "Mummy wasn't just delivering a boring lecture; there was truth in what she said."

We all face different kinds of challenges in our lives. Very few people are lucky to sail through life without weathering any storms. What I realised is this: when those storms rage in your life, life would like you to grab it by its horns and give it a big shake. If you can do that, you are not going to go down. Yes, don't run away, don't cow down. Instead, face it and take action. Do something because your destiny is in your hands. It's all about how you react to a situation. It's your choice. And how *you* react shapes *your* reality. You can either give up or you could choose to shake the horns and emerge victorious. They say you live only once. If so, show the world what you are made of; don't let others tell you who you are or decide for you. You are your best friend; no one will love you more than you can love yourself.

Chapter 12
Soaring with the Angels

Once I had finished with university, there was pressure from Mother and my sisters to return home, so I could get married to a 'suitable' boy. This is typical of Indian society. In my case, at least I was fortunate to have been allowed to pursue my graduation. Even today, so many women are not given access to education. Or they study till high school and are then married off. You see, marriage is the ultimate goal for women in India. Unless you are married, you are not respectable. You need to be 'settled'. Society has changed from those days, but only in urban areas, and that too in liberal families. Otherwise, even in the twenty-first century, a woman needs to be married off to the first suitable man. If not, she becomes a burden on the family. A single woman, however successful she is professionally, is looked at with suspicion. People don't think twice about asking personal, rather invasive questions to unmarried women. It is very common for them to have complete strangers asking them why they are still single. How surreal is this? On one hand, Indians are vying to live and travel abroad, showing off their glitzy vacations to exotic foreign lands on their social media accounts. But scratch below the surface of most of these well-heeled Indians, and you will discover their rigidity, their inherent desire to conform, and their blind adherence to tradition. I do not mean to put everyone one in the same bracket. There are people who are compassionate, liberal, and open to change. My anger is directed at the hypocrites, the ones who are shallow and pretend to be cool and hip, while actually, deep down, harbouring a judgmental and bigoted attitude. I'm sorry, but I just do not have any time for such people.

Anyway, I was not going to go the traditional way and tie the knot. I was proud to have completed my graduation and I was unwilling to give up my hard-won freedom to be confined by marriage and the drudgery of dull domesticity. Because I wanted to flourish and show my potential. I wanted to prove to myself, and the people around me, that I am worthwhile. I didn't need a man to support me financially and I most certainly wasn't prepared to keep house for him. I firmly believe that men and women are equal and that both should shoulder the responsibility of a relationship equally.

I was already looking for a job. I had done an advanced course on Microsoft Office during the gap year, when I'd had to drop out of college because of my severe bout of malaria. I was thankful that I had put that year to use productively by learning a new skill, instead of wasting time. I can give myself a pat on my back for grabbing the opportunity to learn and evolve.

As luck would have it, I got a good break in a multinational company. *Did you notice?* This is the first time I've acknowledged that even I can get lucky. This is also living proof of the saying, 'Every cloud has a silver lining'. Well, I don't know about every cloud, but I was content that this particular cloud on my normally grey horizon did indeed have a prized silver lining.

At that time, in India, working for a multinational company was a dream for most, and many aspired for it. Maybe the tables had turned, and I had emerged from the shadows of my past. I was enjoying working, learning Italian, and getting to know new people. The buzz of the workplace and the hectic pace of my job kept me engaged and contented.

This was a time when I discovered that I have another talent. I realised that not only did I have a penchant for languages, I also had the skill for picking them up. I took up the challenge and topped the class—more kudos.

My success at the workplace buoyed my confidence and I was in a good place. My friends—the real ones—were truly happy for me. The icing on the cake was that I was earning good money as well. And I also had a chance to travel abroad. What more could I ask for? I'd led such a sheltered life. I had hardly travelled on planes or seen much of my own country. And there I was, starting to jet off to exotic destinations. Suddenly, I felt as if I was leading a fairy-tale existence. It was all a bit surreal. I mean, who would believe that

I—this reticent survivor of so much trauma, someone who had attempted to take her life just a couple of years back, someone who lacked self-esteem—was not just a working professional who was independent but was also earning good money, flourishing in her career, and travelling the world.

I met some very talented and knowledgeable people through my job. I also got very close to one of them. He took me under his wing and introduced me to the joys of Italian food and wine. He invited me to many expatriate parties. I find it difficult to define my relationship with him. Was it love? Was it admiration for each other? Was it a strong attraction? I don't know. But I do know that I was happy, very happy. After all the trauma of my childhood, my illness, the loneliness and rejection I'd faced, it was nice to have someone who cared for me, who paid me attention, who took me out on dates. Suddenly, my life had changed. There was someone for me, someone who I could let my hair down with and enjoy the pleasures of life.

But guess what? Because he was not an Indian, the so-called 'friends' started spreading rumours about me. Again, the dreary saga began. I was once more labelled and called names. I was judged, scrutinised, and condemned.

Who did they think they were? The guardians of society? If they held such a moral high ground, why did they not help me when I was literally crying out for help? They turned their backs on me when I was at my lowest, ostracising me and making me plummet to the depths of despair. They had wanted to show that they were superior to me and knew better.

Fortunately, by then, I had learnt not to let people's opinions of me affect me. But I have to confess that it stung a bit. Years later, I would dream of finding closure for all the unresolved emotions I had with them. I am sure they don't even think about those days, about the devastating effect they had on me with their cruel, thoughtless behaviour. Even as I spill out my emotions while writing, I'm reminded of my spiritual leaders' words: "We come alone, we go alone—life is like a stage; we are all playing our parts in a big drama."

I prospered at work and this inspired me to explore the business aspect of the company, which I found fascinating. So my next step was to enrol for a masters' degree in business administration (MBA). I had to go through a rigorous process of preparation and selection to secure a place in the course. Was it another feather in my cap? Yes, I most certainly believe it was. Each success, each new learning was like a booster shot for me, enhancing my confidence and my shaky self-esteem. Suddenly, I believed in myself. I believed that I could do well, I could succeed, and I could go forward.

These were probably the best two years of my life in Mumbai. The course not only kept me in the city for longer, it also provided me with life skills and the motivation to pursue a career in marketing. And what made it even more meaningful and joyful was that I met this most amazing bunch of people. They were bright, genuine go-getters who were focussed and ambitious but, at the same time, also fun-loving. We were in fact the best batch in the institute. The faculty acknowledged our batch as the one that brought the institute much honour and fame. Many of my classmates went on to become successful entrepreneurs and leaders of well-known companies.

During those years, I learnt to grow out of my shell. Because I had business experience already, I could apply the knowledge I had gained to the course. I didn't take a penny from Mother for my course; I part-funded it and took a loan for the rest. It was such a liberating feeling to be independent. And it shored up my self-worth too. It proved to me that I was not some wilting wallflower. I was a strong woman who could do this all on my own. I felt less isolated during those heady days. Even the darkness that surrounded me, and had been my constant companion for years, seemed to ease during that period, letting in light and much-needed happiness. I felt as if I was flying high in the azure sky with angels as my companions. Yes, it was almost like being in heaven. It was euphoria—something I'd never experienced in my angst-ridden life.

And I was careful. I hung out with my friends and we had great fun. But I never ever opened up to anyone about my ordeal. It was not worth opening up those old wounds. Thankfully, they were not festering then; they were buried deep within while I went about the business of living with a newfound purpose. *Let sleeping dogs lie,* I told myself, and got on with my life.

At the end of the course, I was offered a job abroad with a multinational company. This was based on my merit and my proficiency in learning languages. Earlier, I had never had plans or ambitions of leaving India. But when this job landed in my lap, I decided to take it. If this was what was life had in store for me, then I would go with the flow. Life had presented me with a golden opportunity. It was up to me to grab it and make the most of it. I started to dream about travelling to all the places I had read about so long ago in the borrowed books that I had pored over elatedly during my school days.

Life is not all gloom and doom. There's always that sliver of hope, that opening in the door, that multihued rainbow on the horizon that leads to something better. I have shared this idyllic part of my life as an illustration of how it is still possible to keep going and pick ourselves up no matter what life throws at us. You meet so many people during the journey of life and each one teaches you something. Some help you, some reject you, some cheat you, some love you. Each situation and experience is a stepping-stone in your learning curve. We all have our own unique talents and skills. If we identify them, work hard, and do whatever we have to, we can achieve our dreams. It dawned on me that I needed to stand up for myself. I needed to do what I wanted. I needed to reclaim myself. And once I had discovered my strengths, life fell into place, at least in my professional life. And after having been battered by society for so long, this was like manna from heaven for me.

Living outside of India also opened my eyes to other things. I have seen the levels of support and resources available to young people who are victims of physical or sexual abuse. In India, this is still in a nascent stage. The facilities are few and far between. To make matters worse, since society is still so rigid, patriarchal, closeted, and judgemental, the victims are afraid to approach anyone due to the fear of shaming themselves or their families. I urge victims of abuse or CSA to empower themselves by doing something to break the cycle of abuse. If there are no facilities in your area, go online and get yourself self-help books. You can read books and articles about how others have dealt with the trauma. You could also join a forum with like-minded people to share your story with others. It is very redemptive to be part of a community that understands you, empathises with you, and has gone through experiences similar to what you have. You realise you are not alone and you find some sort of peace in shared bonds within that community. Additionally, you often get to hear and read about famous and not-so-famous people sharing their experience and you have that eureka moment when you can understand what the other person is going through because you are sailing on the same boat. One young female golf player shared how she almost gave up her dreams of becoming a star in her field because of how worthless she felt owing to the deep scars that CSA had etched on her. The wounds that any form of abuse leave on us are deep. We may heal, but the scars remain for life. This should also serve as a revelation for society that a perpetrator should never ever be left unpunished. No human being has the right to cause lifelong harm and trauma to another. Most rape and abuse survivors suffer from post-traumatic stress disorder (PTSD) and it can incapacitate a person and leave them distressed and broken for life. Many are never able to pick up the pieces and make themselves whole again—such is the level of suffering they have gone through. You can fix a broken vase and tape it together but if you pour water into the vase, it will leak through the cracks. That's how survivors of abuse are— we are broken and patched up, but the cracks remain.

Being a victim of abuse and having survived it, and also opening myself up to the world with this book, I plead with you that if you happen to be one of those unfortunate souls who is suffering, please get as much help as you can. Be selfish because it is *you* that matters. Remember, no one will be there for you in your darkest hours if you do not stand up for yourself. And that is far, far worse than the shaming. I'd like to add one more important point—*never ever blame yourself or allow others to blame you.* What happened to you is *not* your fault. Once you realise that, and once you are able to share your story, you will find liberation. It will come at a price, a heavy emotional price. But living the truth will give you wings to lead a better life.

Chapter 13
A Different World

Life was never meant to be simple. I guess that's true for everyone. But after all that I have gone through, I seriously believe that, especially for me, life is fraught with challenges, changes, surprises, and more. There I was, enjoying life, finally forging a path of independence and revelling in the freedom to live life on my own terms. I was flushed with joy—I had a job I loved, I was earning well, I had great friends, I was travelling and imbibing new cultures and new knowledge. My life was on an upward trajectory.

And then, my life took a different turn.

I had to start life all over again. I had to move to the UK. It was a different world altogether, and I struggled to cope with the change and forge new friendships, while facing rejection as I strove to make a fresh start in my career…

Why did I move to UK? Well, I could only fight the coercion to get married for so long. Apparently, I was not doing great, or rather, not fulfilling my 'duty' as a 'good Indian girl' if I did not bag a husband before I—horror of horrors—crossed into my late twenties. Then,

I would be 'on the shelf', with my prospects of bagging a 'good' husband narrowing down with each passing year.

With all this pressure to conform, I finally gave in to the constant barrage of Mother's pleas to accept the idea of marriage. The whole thing was wearing me down. She was very keen on finding me a suitable husband. In India, the community—family, friends and well-meaning neighbours—pitch in to help find a suitable groom. He has to belong to the same community and caste, and usually comes recommended by close friends or family.

Was I keen on marriage? No. I think I made that quite clear in the previous chapter. But on some level, I felt obliged to succumb to the pressure of leading a conventional life and doing what was expected of me.

Honestly, the most compelling reason was Mother I didn't want to upset her after all that she had done for me. I was very conflicted. There was the unbridled joy of living life on your own terms, but always with this underlying guilt that you had failed your family. And then there was marriage—a gamble at the best of times. It would mean sacrificing my newfound freedom, but it would also mean that I would make Mother happy. I had long, knotty conversations with a couple of my close and trusted friends as I tried to gain clarity on what I should do. My friends felt that it was worth it, that I should give marriage a try.

I struggled with my feelings. This was not an easy decision—to give up everything that I loved for something I had no affinity towards. But I have this sense of undying loyalty towards my mother owing to all the sacrifices she has made for me. Hers had never been an easy life, especially after losing her husband at such a young age. She had struggled to bring up six daughters on her own. She had given in to my pleas to send me to an English medium school. And had agreed to send me to Mumbai even though, deep down, her conservative mindset was not in agreement with my actions. My family and community, which were inherently conservative, were not happy when I left for Mumbai, and she was left to handle the aftermath of that and bear the gaze of displeasure from her community.

After all, in a patriarchal setup, a girl didn't need to educate herself so much. All she required was basic education. After that, her lot in life was to be married off. Who needed all these fancy degrees when the ultimate aim in life for a girl was to get hitched? Subsumed in the daily rhythms of domesticity—cooking, cleaning, and taking care of all the needs of the family—a degree was useless. And after marriage, the next duty of a woman is to produce a male heir. Once she has done this, she has circumscribed to societal expectations and is looked upon as a 'good wife'.

I was overwhelmed with guilt. I felt as if I was being extraordinarily selfish in turning a deaf ear to Mother's implorations, especially when all the other daughters had done as she asked. So many thoughts whirled inside my head. She had, after all, educated me in a big city—an opportunity my other siblings were not afforded—so wasn't that all the more reason that I should agree to her pleas and make her happy?

I sorely missed a strong male figure; I so missed my father. If he had been alive, I could have approached him for advice and asked him if he saw me fitting into an arranged marriage. Maybe if he had been around, my mother would not have had to bear the weight of society's expectations or the glare of disapproval from her community. There were so many times when I was growing up that I missed my father; the lack of a paternal figure to guide and protect us remained within me like a festering wound. Would my abuser have had so much access to our family, and therefore me, if my father had been around? Mother was brought up in a patriarchal society and got married early—I knew she herself was a victim of patriarchy. So, how could I expect her to not have the same expectations of me? Having a daughter is a curse in Indian society; my poor mother had six daughters! And unless and until each one was married and settled, the lens of society would look upon her censoriously.

Also, I must confess that I have this inherent weakness to please everyone. So, apart from feeling guilty about her sacrifices, my desire to please also played a role in my agreeing to get married. This is a side of me that I am not particularly fond of. I give in easily because, most often, I feel that my voice doesn't count. It's probably an insidious influence of my tormented childhood.

Looking back, I realise that sanity must have flown out of my head. I was foolish to have overridden my own reservations. I gave up like a weakling and, finally, during a work trip to Italy, I agreed to visit my would-be husband's parents in the UK so as to be introduced to their son. I was not in the least bit excited; instead, I was very apprehensive—understandably so. But I was also playing this subtle game. On the outside, I had succumbed; I had agreed to get married. But, in reality, deep within me, I was not prepared to give up everything and tie the matrimonial knot. I thought that if I outwardly agreed and met the family, when it didn't work out, it would get Mother off my back. As per my logic, I couldn't fathom how a boy brought up in a western country would agree to marry a girl straight off a plane from India. So I was pretty sure he would reject me. Then, I could fly back to India and resume my life and career in Mumbai.

Nevertheless, life takes strange twists and turns, and the unexpected happens. Much to my surprise, meeting my would-be husband and his family seemed like a dream come true. I had met them before at family gatherings when I was much younger. They didn't feel like strangers to me; on the contrary they were very loving and welcomed me, making me feel as if I was a part of their family. They seemed liberal, hospitable, and caring. This sense of relief washed over me. I felt I could be myself, and that life was taking a good turn. I found what I had missed while growing up—a family, a real family with a mother and a father, a family who paid attention to me. With Father gone and Mother always concerned about how to make ends meet, she was unable to give her daughters the time and attention they needed while growing up. My ex-husband's mother, apart from being caring towards me, is highly educated, well-spoken, and also had a career; this appealed to me immensely.

I enjoyed the company of his parents. They were urbane, sophisticated, and well-travelled; they socialised in elite circles. This was something I'd always craved as a child, but growing up in a small town, struggling for money and the good things in life, this was a life I had never seen.

The parents enfolded me in the warmth of their care, pampering me as if I was their own daughter. I was seeing life through a different prism. It was all so new and wondrous to me. They took me out sightseeing and shopping and showered me with attention.

I felt as if God had mandated that they come into my life, to give me a taste of the things that my life had lacked earlier—a father and a mother, a family that was sophisticated, well off, worldly, and sociable.

Mother, you see, as much as I love her as she is, never had any exposure to the world outside her village and her town. She was comfortable in her parochial existence, and as kids, our exposure was limited to our small town and the circumscribed world of our equally parochial neighbours. I do believe that Mother would have attained her true potential, given the opportunity, because she was inherently astute and intelligent. However, sadly, her circumstances never gave her a chance to break out of the confines of patriarchy and tradition. Please understand, I am not judging Mother. I am merely observing and conveying the reality of what so many of my peers had with their parents, which I didn't. That's all.

My ex-husband's parents had settled in the southwest of England. They had merged into the society there and had an extensive circle of friends who they mingled with regularly. Even though they had been living in England for a long time, they still cherished their roots and spoke to me in my mother tongue, which, along with their kindly attitude, helped me to feel completely at home.

When I visited, it was summer, a time when England is at its glorious best with buttery sunshine bathing the streets in a golden glow. Life appeared to be good. I thought to myself when all this was happening, that even if their son didn't like me, I was fortunate to have been able to visit this beautiful country and get to spend time with this loving couple. It was as if a gap that I had been trying to fill had not only been filled to the brim but was overflowing.

Now what can I say about the man I was to marry? I bowled him over! He was enthralled by me, he thought the world of me, he wouldn't let go of me. And as for me... well, I liked him. He appeared to be a good-natured, witty young man. He was also very musically talented and that was something I really admired in him. In spite of all my apprehensions, we hit it off well. We started courting—or that's how I saw it because things were happening very fast. It was as if I was caught up in a dizzying whirlwind. I was swept off my feet with everything around me—a new country, a new culture, new people, loving attention, and, most importantly, the weight of this huge impending change in my life.

We were out sightseeing in London one day, when he proposed to me. I still remember the day so clearly. We had just visited the National Art Gallery, where we had admired many paintings and exchanged our views on them; we even joked about a few of them. He didn't have a ring with him as he had not planned on proposing that day. It was all so very sudden and spontaneous. And rather dramatic, like something out of a movie. All of a sudden, he went down on his knee and announced to everyone around that his proposal to marry me had been accepted. I was totally taken aback; I was in a state of shock. Could I have said no? That I needed time to think? Well, I didn't, and from thereon, my life took a turn I hadn't anticipated. He was so overjoyed when I accepted that he called his brother and his best friend, who were also taken by surprise at this sudden development.

If I thought I'd been caught up in a whirlwind, well, now it seemed as if I was in the middle of a superfast vortex. Or on an escalator without a stop button. Everything was spinning rapidly now, totally out of my control.

He called Mother and asked for my hand. It goes without saying that Mother and my sisters were overjoyed. They had always wished the best for me and, for them, this was the best thing that could happen to me.

There was a flurry of activities now that he had formally proposed. Preparations for the wedding started immediately. The date was set, invitations were printed and sent out, and the family house was given a pristine, fresh coat of paint. It was a time for celebration—the youngest daughter was getting married to an eligible boy from the UK. (In India, marrying a man abroad is very high on the pecking order of desirable alliances.) She was meant to have this as she was well educated and beautiful. Unlike my peers, I never thought it necessary to find out how much my fiancé earned. Since I was working and earning well, I was determined to contribute my fair share once we married. I didn't expect to sit back and expect my husband to provide for us. After all, I hadn't gone on to get an MBA for nothing.

The wedding date was fixed for within six months of me visiting the UK. In between, my fiancé came to visit me in Mumbai, giving me the opportunity to introduce him to my friends. He was easy-going and embraced Mumbai's culture, which was reassuring for me because I loved what the city had to offer. He got on well with my friends, all of whom had been brought up in India, and enjoyed their company. I got to spend time with him in my own environment, which was important to me because I needed to know how he would fit into my milieu.

The wedding was held in my hometown Guwahati. I am so tempted to skip this part as I find it difficult to revisit those times in detail. It's a feeling I cannot describe. If I tried, the closest I can come to expressing it is that it was as if it was another life. Life is so extraordinary, so unpredictable. We had been so happy then, filled with hope and gazing ecstatically at the world with rose-tinted glasses. Then, why did it not work out? Well...

Preparing for the wedding was so much fun. I had a great time going shopping with my sisters for clothes and jewellery. My sisters knew I was very picky and had an eye for fashion, so they let me select the gifts they were getting for me too. This was the only wedding in the family which was not held in the premises of Mother's home. Was it an omen? Yes, I am superstitious enough to think so.

The venue was chosen by my uncle and it was the best we could get. It was a grand wedding and we had gone to town on the décor and food for the thousand plus guests over two days of celebrations. People said I was the most beautiful bride they had seen, and the wedding and my beauty were buzzing topics of conversation during those times. The two days of wedding festivities kept us all busy. There was so much hustle and bustle in the house, and all the sadness of the past was forgotten. It was like a festival. We remembered Father, as we always do on special occasions. His younger brother gave my hand away as he had done for the rest of my sisters. I enjoyed having my hair and makeup done; I posed for photos with family and friends, danced with the guests, and revelled in the celebrations. I had invited my schoolteachers because I'd always had a strong affinity for my school and cherished the days I'd spent there. And of course, my school friends were part of the celebrations too. I still have the photos of the wedding, because one day, my son might want to see them. We had my ex-husband's friends and family visit from all over the world.

In those days, there was a lot of unrest in Assam, and incidents of terrorism in the state had made national headlines. As a result, my friends from Mumbai, who were still young, were not given permission by their parents to travel the long distance that it was to Assam to attend a wedding in a strife-torn region. I missed them but I later threw a party for them in Mumbai. We had a rocking time; we danced the night away, and finally, exhausted but happy, we staggered out onto the empty roads and found a roadside food joint where we hungrily gulped down some delicious street food. I have fond memories to look back on even though things didn't go as I had dreamt they would.

I was sad to leave my country and my friends to live abroad. Unlike most of my contemporaries, I had never aspired to go overseas to forge my future. I was content with my life and happy with my job and friends in Mumbai.

The thrill and the anticipation of a new life comes coupled with its own fears and uncertainties. I had to leave behind job offers in India and Italy, options I could no longer consider. My husband was already settled in the UK, so there was no question of him moving to India or Italy. I had to start a new life with him in the UK, which I believed was going to be just fine. After all, everything seemed perfect. I had in-laws who had received me with open arms into their family and a husband who was head over heels in love with me. Life held a fistful of delightful promises for me, and I was willing to believe that I was leaving the pain of my tormented past behind for something beautiful, something precious...

Chapter 14
Living Life on My Own Terms

Being a single mother is tough. Often, I was vulnerable to being judged. It was as if I gave strangers an open invitation to ask me questions that were deeply personal to me. It wasn't so bad in Europe but would happen quite often when I travelled outside the continent. And it happened more often than I liked it to. I felt compelled to stand up for myself while trying not to hide who I am. There was no reason to hide the real me or feel as if I was some kind of anomaly. I had not done anything wrong. But I must confess that all that unwarranted probing and the judgemental looks did make me feel odd and intensely uncomfortable. There's something dreadfully invasive about people asking you questions that are so personal. It truly is none of their business, but they make it their business.

In Asia, where patriarchy is embedded into the system, it's very common for perfect strangers to ask, "Where is your husband? Why is he not here with you on holiday?" I want to scream out and say, "Why don't you mind your own business!" But I grit my teeth and control myself. Instead, I tell myself, "They do not know any different, and who cares what they think."

What I do know is that I'd rather be on my own than be miserable in a failed marriage. In Asia, and in my home country India, so many women are trapped in marriages that are unhappy or lacking in love. I don't judge them. The women who stay on in these unhappy unions have their reasons. It could be that they lack financial dependence or that they fear the social stigma of being labelled a divorcee.

My advice to such women—and I do not mean to preach because I speak from my own experience—is to break free. Life is too short to live it ensnared in fear and misery. Don't be afraid to stand alone. Your children may not understand your stance or decision when they are young, but they will thank you for it one day.

I still recall how I felt tears well up once—when my son said that he understood why I had taken the steps I did. They were tears of happiness. You see, it does not matter what the people with wagging tongues say; they are not there for you when you need support. What really matters is how your loved ones feel about you, as their love is unconditional. For me, that is my son. I stand strong because I know I have his love and support. I know he is there for me. I know he will be there for me. He is my comfort and my solace. The gossips and the slanderers, the curious and the nosy, just want to poke and probe into my life. They need something to talk about, to point at, to feel morally righteous about. All this, while they live a life of pretence and lead their dull, circumscribed lives in servitude to society and a desperate attempt to put a veil on their sad reality. I may not have a husband. But I am independent and free. And I have the greatest thing I could wish for in my life—my precious son, who loves me, admires me, and respects me.

So, when I am faced with an uncomfortable situation, where people ask me probing questions about my life, I dig deep inside me to find the calm that I have worked so hard to find. I smile sweetly as I do not owe anyone an explanation. I just say that I am here on holiday with my son while my husband is working to pay for it. My son looks at me and gives me a knowing wink. We have a good laugh about it later.

I often wonder: have other single mothers who are not victims of CSA felt the same way I do? Or was it due to my feelings of low self-esteem and self-worth that I felt that I am lacking? I read many books by psychologists who have studied the minds of various CSA victims. And owing to that, I have realised that most CSA victims will develop post-traumatic stress disorder (PTSD). The fear, the feelings of worthlessness, and the low moods become an intrinsic part of who we are, and it takes a lot of work to overcome this. By 'work', I mean talk therapy and medication, with the guidance and care of professionals.

I have gone through the journey of self-discovery—to understand myself, my feelings, my reactions, the moods and the patterns that repeat themselves. This has helped me to gain a deep awareness of myself and my condition. Do you know what the most important thing I discovered was that helped me overcome my own demons? That it is our thoughts that make us feel the way we do. We, the victims of CSA, blame ourselves for no fault of our own. We feel inadequate; we felt helpless when we were children and that feeling never leaves us; so, we continue to feel that same sense of helplessness when we navigate the world as adults. I have always looked for someone else—a grown-up—to resolve any issue for me, be it be at work or at home. I always felt incapable of handling issues on my own. There was always this fear that I would do things wrong. There was a reticence to take the bull by the horns and tackle my own issues. I constantly needed someone else because I had no faith in my own abilities. Somewhere, that little child who had undergone so much trauma, still lurked below the veneer of adulthood.

Learning to stand on my own feet and embracing my true self was a long and hard journey. But with the help of my spiritual leader and medical professionals, I have learnt invaluable techniques for self-help. They opened my eyes to so many realities. And one of the most invaluable lessons I learnt was that all through my life I have been able to help myself. I understood that I do not need to feel the paralysing fear I did as a child—

when I was abused and desperately seeking an adult to come to my rescue.

Through the lens of this new knowledge, I recognised that, as an adult, I can help myself in the same way that I help my son. After all, any mother knows how dependent a child is on her. The child learns to navigate the world through the comfort and succour he or she gets from the love of his or her mother. The mother is the pillar of support; the mother is the nurturer; the mother will sacrifice anything for the happiness of her child. We put our child's needs before our own. I understood that I do have the reserve and strength within me; it's just that it got buried in the debris of my childhood ordeal. I rose like a phoenix from the ashes to start a new life with a new me.

Let me tell you, the entire process was far from easy. You need a lot of practice and patience with yourself. I decided it was time for me to start loving myself for who I am. I made a promise to myself to check my thoughts. When my mind or my own moods would let me down, I'd rein them back to the present moment—to a space where, I reminded myself, I am free and there is no fear. I resolved to live in the moment. All I needed to do was appreciate and absorb the natural beauty around me. I told myself that I would not allow my thoughts to rule my head before I validated them and understood whether they are true and real. It took time; it took a lot of effort. After having lived in fear, after having tormenting thoughts swirl through my mind like an unwelcome guest all through my life, changing that embedded pattern was a herculean task. But slowly, over time, things started to change for the better. Soon, it became a habit—my second nature. All I needed to do was to stick with this and to live in the present moment.

The Buddha said, *Do not dwell on the past. Do not dream of the future. Concentrate the mind on the present moment.* Today, that is a mantra I live by. Living in the moment helps you to focus on your current life and appreciate the blessings you have. It helps you to shrug off the seductive but dangerous pull of the past. It helps you to stay grounded and not worry about the future. The present moment is all we have. We need to cherish it, embrace it, savour it. I've realised that I can't change my past. I can cry over it, gnash my teeth, and rage at the injustice of it all. But it has happened and there's nothing that will change the solid reality of that. What I can change is only myself and my living reality. And to do that, I need to pay attention to the present and open my arms to the wealth of love and opportunities that I have been blessed with and thank God for all my blessings. The past is a stain that will probably inhabit the deepest recesses of my soul. But I don't have to let the past define my present and define who I am. I deserve happiness and living in the moment helps me to appreciate the joys of life and define and love my current self. I have decided to make every moment of my life count.

The what ifs, the should-haves, the what would Mother say, what would Sister say, what would the neighbours say… is all nonsense and totally inconsequential. The mind shift to think differently does not happen instantly, as I said earlier, but today, I do not break the promise I made to myself. I practise the techniques I have been equipped with. It is also about working with myself; it is about being gentle and kind to myself. Amongst the techniques that I learnt, I found the breathing exercises to be the most helpful. I have this tendency of reacting in a knee-jerk fashion to situations unfolding around me. I would never think before acting or speaking; my reactions would be spontaneous… and often the wrong way to respond. I have discovered that taking a pause to breathe before I react helps me to check myself from countering inappropriately or upsetting myself over things—people or situations— that I have no control over.

If what I have said resonates with you, or if you are in a similar situation and feel you are lacking in resources to help you, there are many ways to help yourself. For starters, you can look up videos online which guide you with meditation techniques. There are several charitable organisations that you can reach out to as well. You could also check out apps for meditation and wellness; there are so many. The internet is a blessing and a tool we can appropriate for our road to wellness. I encourage you to make a start today. I am with you in spirit—your comrade in your journey towards self-realisation, and in your battles with yourself and your surroundings.

For many of you who are victims of abuse or suffer from low self-esteem, you may find it difficult to believe me. You may think that life is hopeless or that you cannot stand up and fight for your right to be yourself. You may doubt that it is even remotely possible. Well, I am living proof that it *is* possible. I will prove it to you by sharing more about me, my life, and the challenges I faced. We don't need to get so caught up in regrets of the past that we prevent ourselves from blossoming in the future.

I survived. I may have been drowning but I reached out for a life jacket and, gasping and struggling, I came up for air, and not only survived but thrived. Today, I don't just exist. I am no longer merely a victim. I had the courage to reframe and reshape my perspective on life. I am a strong, beautiful woman who believes in herself and stands up for herself. I am a proud single mother who no longer cares what society has to say about her. I may have been the girl who should have been a boy. But now, I am me and I'm happy to inhabit that space and live life on my own terms.

Chapter 15
A Conspiracy against Me?

Was it a wise decision to get married on an impulse? Did I allow myself to indulge in my burning desire to run as far as I could from my hometown in my quest for light?

I wish I could time travel to look into the future, as I lack the gift of thinking things through. I also suffer from the 'yes' syndrome. It's not something I am proud of, because I detest any form of weakness in myself.

At that time, I never saw any reason not to get married to this man who I saw as an easy-going, happy-go-lucky person. I was not totally bowled over by his looks, but I thought I glimpsed a good heart in him. He seemed like someone who would not hurt me. After all the pain and rejection, loneliness and isolation, and the terrible experiences I had suffered, I desperately wanted to believe that I had found security and could escape from India, a country that, to me, was a repository of nightmarish occurrences. He didn't know about my painful truth then. I couldn't tell him. How could I? I was paralyzed by a cold fear. Fear that he would look at me with contempt, that he would think it was my fault, that he would think I was 'damaged goods', that he would walk away…

These thoughts kept swirling in my head—the guilt of not telling him and the urge to tell him… to purge myself of the heavy weight of my ugly truth, to come clean, wipe the slate, and begin life afresh. If he knew the truth, I would be unburdened, unfettered, and we could start our life without the baggage of my truth. I would be lighter and freer, and our relationship would begin on a solid foundation of truth and trust.

But alas, by now it was too late. We were engaged. The families were very happy about the match and starting to look at auspicious dates. In India, you don't get married on any day. Astrologers are consulted to select a propitious date based on the horoscopes of both the bride and the groom to select a day when the stars are aligned favourably for the couple.

With all this flurry of excitement and joy surging around me, I did not have the heart to blanket the happiness of my family's and his with the darkness of my reality. I shuddered to think of the consequences of coming clean. So, I buried my head in the sand. I started to believe that things would be different, that my life would no longer be part darkness part light. I believed that we could start afresh, where the light and sunshine of new beginnings would eclipse the blackness of my past.

My fiancé was happy and in love with me. He was always eager to see me, so he visited me in Mumbai after I returned to complete my course. I liked his outgoing nature. I was also quite touched by his childlike enthusiasm to visit India, the country of his origin.

I still remember one of his visits. It was during the time of the Ganpati celebrations in Mumbai. The city was dotted with beautifully decorated *puja pandals*. Ganpati *puja* is a time when the city comes alive, when the roads swell with people celebrating the beloved elephant god. There is something so magical about it... pretty *pandals* bedecked with flowers and lights, the hypnotic rhythm of drums, music wafting through the air, and the happy faces of people milling around as they partake in the festivities.

I thought we were in love and believed that this is what love was. I thanked him for bringing joy and radiance into my life, just like Ganpati brought joy and light into the lives of Mumbaikars and brought colour to the city. At that time, in that atmosphere of festive celebration, when there was so much joie-de-vivre around, I envisioned a bright future, a time of happiness and peace with this man by my side, a time when I could forget my traumatic past and actually savour the sweet joy of love. I couldn't foresee a time when he would turn around and tell me that he never loved me, that he had just been blinded.

Blinded by what, I ask myself? I never had or will consider myself to be some beauty queen. I consider myself average owing to my dark complexion, as compared to my sisters. You see, in India, we are as racist as people are in the West. Colour matters. Men and their families want a 'fair bride' and I was far from fair. And my sisters were definitely prettier than me; I'd always felt like the ugly duckling amongst them. The monster used to tell me that I looked too skinny or too dark or that my face was dull. He stole everything from me along with my self-respect. It was not enough for him to have plundered my body and thereby seared my soul, but he also took away my self-esteem. I believed I was ugly, worthless, unlovable. In my childhood innocence, I thought that being molested and pawed by the brute was punishment for being ugly.

Not everything leading to the wedding was rosy. I still ask myself: *Could I have saved myself from the grief I would face in future?* My fiancé came to pick me up from Mumbai on his way to our common hometown where the wedding was to be held. Only six months had passed since we had got to know each other. It was early yet to have a lover's tiff. Nonetheless, we had a row over some trivial matter. He later told me that he had wanted to turn back then. I wish he had told me about this. Maye then, we wouldn't have got married and lived an unhappy union

Suddenly, I was brought back to the present by the loud, joyous laughter of a bunch of boys. Coming back to my senses, I realised that not marrying him would have meant that I wouldn't have had my child, who is the most precious being to me in this world.

I look at my beautiful son, the light of my life, watching a movie and eating chocolate, trying desperately not to get it on his T-shirt because the chocolate has melted due to the heat. The chocolate has left gooey, chocolatey stains on his T-shirt. I look at his innocent face absorbed in the movie and my heart constricts. There is an outpouring of love and gratitude. I can't imagine my life without him. I can't imagine not being a mum to him, my most precious gift of all. That bad marriage was worth it all just for this—my beautiful, beautiful boy. I wouldn't have it any other way.

I am responsible for this beautiful human being. I brought him into this world and he changed my world, making it better and giving me hope. It is my responsibility to make a good man out of him. I chide myself for doubting myself and promise to believe in myself like my good friends keep urging me to do.

My friends are fooling around with each over a game of cards. It reminds me of my days in Mumbai—the friends, the warmth, and the laughter that I left behind when I moved to the UK. A surge of nostalgia for chaotic Mumbai rises in me. The city of dreams, the city of contrasts—where glittering skyscrapers stand cheek-by-jowl with crowded slums. It's a city that signifies the dichotomy of life—of wealth and poverty, of joy and sorrow, of black and white with shades of grey in between. But above all, it speaks of resilience and the beauty of hope. That tomorrow could be a better day. That this misery need not be a lifelong condition. It is the city of dreams and its ethos resonates with me. I can dream and hope for a better future too.

I have come a long way from the broken, wounded person that I was but I acknowledge that there is still a lot of longing and pain I need to learn to overcome in order to find contentment in the 'here and now', as one of my therapists had instilled in me. But I know I'm growing, I know I'm evolving, I know that tomorrow comes with a promise of something better. Just like chaotic Mumbai, my mind swirls with a labyrinth of emotions, of impossible juxtapositions, of giddy highs and devastating lows... but tomorrow is another day.

Slowly, I am learning to live in the present and put the shadow of the past behind me. And writing this book has helped me in that cathartic journey. With my adorable son in my life, the love of my partner, the joy and warmth of close friends, and a strong belief in myself, I rise phoenix-like, knowing that I can take on the future with resilience and a more zen-like calm. Yes, I am washed of my 'sins', I am cleansed, and I look forward to the challenges that life will throw my way. I am proud and confident of who I am. I may have been the girl who should have been a boy... but today, I love the woman I am.

Hope is important because it can make the present moment less difficult to bear. If we believe that tomorrow will be better, we can bear a hardship today.
　—Thich Nhat Hanh

Chapter 16
Life as We 'Don't' Know It

My marriage began and ended with the honeymoon; at least that's what it felt like to me. The rosiness of the first few months, the smiles, hugs, and all those tiny but meaningful gestures and looks that signalled love remained trapped in the photo albums that we'd created as a testament to our new beginnings. The colour faded away from my cheeks and my smiles turned into sorrow. Hope gave way to gloom and despair... My dreams had been shattered and the shards that surrounded me could never be fixed and whole again.

If the marriage front was all doom and gloom, my career too seemed to have no silver lining in the initial days of my move to England. I had never expected my future in a new country to be a bed of roses but neither had I expected it to be an ordeal. I had left behind lucrative job offers in India only to have to do the rounds of recruitment agencies. In those days, there weren't too many online job sites. I would trudge down to the city centre where the agencies were located and fill in the registration forms. I would look around for a familiar face, a smile, someone to have a coffee with. But the only person I knew in the city was my husband.

England is a country where it can rain at any time and this was something I was not used to. I'd find myself cold or wet on my way home because I so often misjudged the weather. This was before smartphones had come along to make our lives easier to plan with weather forecast apps.

Life was quite a drudgery. I was either visiting agencies to look for work or would be cooped up in our one-bedroom waterfront house that we were renting then. With plenty of time on my hands and no friends that I could hang out with, the highlight of my day was waiting for my husband to come home from work, which he did straight back from the office, unless he was playing a round of golf after. Otherwise, I would pass my time looking out of the window and soaking in the views from there. There was a constant flow of people going past—runners, joggers, mums with prams, and dog walkers. But it was lonely, terribly lonely. An alien country and an alien culture. I was alone all day and longed for the warmth of human company, of loved ones, of friends. I missed India... its chaos, noise, hustle-bustle, and crowds.

The nights were even lonelier even though my husband was with me. Our marriage lacked passion. I would feel pangs of envy when I heard our neighbours making love. I yearned to be touched, to be hugged, to be kissed, to make love—normal things that any marriage should entail. However, at that time, I never felt there was anything wrong with us. But now, looking back, I am able to see that everything was wrong as we never connected on an intimate level. If only twenty-twenty vision was not limited to hindsight.

But we continued to live together in what we believed was a fairly normal married life. He was quite set in his ways and found compromise difficult. He would sometimes tell me that marriage made one give up things they were passionate about, like the Sundays when he played cricket. No wonder he never forgave me for having to give up his band when we decided to move to London because of my career.

And I was quite naïve and vulnerable. I actually believed it when someone told me that married people didn't have sex unless they were trying for a baby. I was able to shrug off our lack of intimacy as a result of my gullibility. I never realised that sex, making love, physical intimacy... were all intrinsic to a happy, fulfilling marriage.

Thankfully, after a few false starts, I finally made headway in my career and found something that was right up my alley. I was very excited to start this new chapter in our lives. Apart from the lack of physical intimacy, we did get on and could even share a few laughs. We travelled the world together. Friends and family saw us as a happy couple. Typical of Indians, we were often subjected to eager inquisitions about when we were planning on having a child. We hadn't really thought about a baby—about whether we should have one or not. It was one of those things we hadn't really thought about or spoken about. It was as if we had left it to fate. I was not on contraception as I didn't need it, owing to the lack of activity in our bedroom.

I enjoyed living and working in London. I put my heart and soul into my career and was doing very well and being acknowledged for my contributions. We had a lovely home in a middleclass suburb, which cost us more than double that of the previous house. But we could afford it. My husband had got a well-paid job in the city too.

I guess it was the sense of fulfilment and being relaxed with where we were in life that changed something in us. We resumed our lovemaking and just that one time we were showered with something precious, someone precious, who would become the centre of our lives.

My pregnancy was an easy one. I managed to travel back to India to see my family, who were, naturally, overjoyed with the news. I even made a long-haul trip to the West Indies to watch the World Cup cricket with friends. This was a trip that had been planned before I became pregnant and with everything going well, the doctor gave me the all clear to travel. He was not entirely happy that I was taking a risk so late into the pregnancy but, thankfully for me, he somehow gave in. We were in the sunny West Indies, enjoying the weather, the hospitality, and the sport. Everything went well and we had a marvellous time. It helped to have my close friend with me. We drank freshly squeezed sugarcane juice (a luxury) while the others enjoyed their tipple.

There was not much time for baby to arrive after we got back from the trip. Mother was coming for the birth (her first trip abroad) with my eldest nephew. I was happy and content. I felt as if, with the arrival of the baby, I would be reborn. I felt awash with hope. I thought the baby would change everything, perhaps even give our marriage a new lease of life. The baby would bring my husband and me together and we would live as a cosy, happy family. I would no longer be lonely because my baby would be there to enrich my life.

I was not in the least bit worried about a minor complication that the doctor had told me could arise during birth. I was positive that everything was going to be all right. At home, we had lovingly designed our baby's nursery and it was all ready to welcome him. The midwife had given me a list of things I needed for the hospital and homecoming, and we had ensured that everything was ready.

We arrived at the hospital on the day set for the C-section nice and early, waiting for my time to be taken into the theatre. They had to clear a couple of cases from the previous day. I felt quite relieved that I was not going to have a normal birth when I heard the screams of the women in labour. I was filled with energy, hope and excitement as I lay there waiting my turn. I was trying to will them to wheel me away from the waiting room to the theatre.

In the theatre, time seemed to stand still. I was awake during the procedure and when I felt the local anaesthetic wear off, they gave me another dose. I started to wonder what was going on. Why was the midwife being extra kind? I looked at her askance and she gave me a reassuring smile. In one corner of the room, I saw my husband deep in conversation with a medical team. He was then called to witness the arrival of the baby; the surgeon asked the midwife not to remove the shield so that I would be able to witness it as well. I waited patiently (okay, not that patiently!).

Then came the cry. My child, the only being who would give me the willpower to fight on and live had arrived! My eyes brimmed with tears of joy. The midwife asked the father, who was fussing around and holding the newborn, to bring him over for a feed. Something shifted within me... something deep and moving. I felt as if I had existed for this moment all my life. I now felt that there was a meaning, a *real meaning* to my troubled existence. I forgot about myself; I did not care. When the baby was taken away after his feed, the surgeon came to speak to me. She was wearing a glass shield over her face, which was splattered with blood. She told me that, as she had warned, I had lost a lot of blood. She had done her best not to cut through me too much, which was why it had taken about an hour to get my baby out.

She asked me to rest while she and her colleagues completed their job. Which meant sucking up the litres of blood I had lost and sewing me up. It took them three hours to finish. In the meantime, I was attached to a drip and my blood sample was sent to the lab. I needed an emergency blood transfusion. For the next forty-eight hours, I was under observation and was confined to the bed. All I could do was feed my darling baby. We had named him by then as we had chosen a name already. I was unable to do anything else; that was left to the father and the nurses.

Back at home, Mother and my in-laws were worried sick, not knowing what had happened and wondering why it was taking so long. They were waiting for news, any news. They waited all day. Lunchtime came and went and they waited, not even eating, so anxious were they to know what was happening. Finally, early in the evening, they were given the news of the arrival of a healthy baby boy and were overjoyed. They enjoyed a sumptuous feast for dinner to celebrate the event. They even sent food to the hospital while the nurses looked on with polite disapproval.

I was treated like a princess when I got home. I had the luxury of resting in my room. Food and beverages were sent to me and my mother and in-laws took over all the baby duties. My in-laws returned to their home after a few days, Mother stayed with us for quite a while to look after me and baby. My near-death experience had shaken her and she was extremely worried. She wanted me to stay in bed till I recovered. I explained to her that, unlike in India, mothers were up and about a week after delivery and did not have the luxury of languishing in bed for weeks or months. I wish though that I had not been so direct and upfront with her; I wish I had explained this to her more gently. Like I said earlier, there is nothing like hindsight…

Chapter 17
A New Mum and Beyond

The train to the office in central London was a short walk from our home. My heart used to sing and swell with joy along with the spring blossoms in the gardens at the imminent arrival of baby. I was looking forward to having Mother over—the first time anyone from my family would be visiting me in my new home country. I made all the arrangements for her visa and her tickets. My heart was filled with pride that I could do this for her. It was a payback with love for her first trip abroad—a small but meaningful gesture for all the sacrifices she had made for me. After all, in spite of her conservative background and her hesitance to send me for further studies, she had overcome it all, had had the courage to stand firm against family who believed that educating a girl too much was a waste of time, and, with her limited means, had done whatever she could to help me get the education I believed I deserved.

It was really a blessing to have Mother over and I loved every moment of having her with us. I enjoyed the sheer, unadulterated joy of eating her simple homemade food, which took me down memory lane to the sights and smells of my childhood in distant Assam. I enjoyed bonding with her one to one, a luxury I had never had in India, because our house was always full—with my siblings and visiting family. We would take baby out for fresh air daily. We followed this routine for the few months she was over. For Mother, England was a new world. She had been cocooned in her own little world in India and suddenly here was something so different, so foreign. She admired the clean streets and beautifully laid out gardens. However, she couldn't understand why I had to do the housework (except the weekly cleaning by paid help) after such a difficult birth. In India, we have household help to take care of daily domestic chores, so this was quite a culture shock for her. Anyway, my time with Mother was beautiful and I truly cherished it. I wish I it could have happened again. But then, I didn't have another child and now Mother's health is fragile, making it difficult for her to embark on long journeys... or so she says.

I tried to give baby the best exposure for his age—taking him to soft play, activity classes, and even on holidays. I remember how excited he was so when he first saw snow and played in the sand on the beach, tasting it to savour the whole experience. Fortunately, he was not a difficult child when we travelled. Whether it was short or long flights, he adapted well. It is as if he was an extension of me. I loved being a mum, I revelled in my new role. The only part I found tough was the sleepless nights, which left me tired and snappy during the day. This was something the husband didn't care to understand.

The tension in the marriage began to build. I was all set to get back to work. I had arranged a nursery for baby and I thought I could strike a good work-life balance. It was a time of recession and my husband had to work away from home. He didn't like the idea of me getting back to full-time work. This made me feel unsettled, as I was already experiencing the guilt a new mum feels when she has to leave her precious child with someone else. But many mums have done both—be a parent and have a career. It was, after all, the twenty-first century.

I tried to talk over the issue over with my employer. I requested that I be given the flexibility of combining working from home and the office. Times were very different then. Unlike now, when work from home (WFH) has become the norm (due to Covid-19), in those days, it was not an accepted practice. It was deemed necessary for me to be in the office to be able to do my work. I was allowed to leave a few minutes early to be able to catch an earlier train by taking a shorter lunch break. I somehow managed with this arrangement. It was going okay but could have been better if only my employer had understood. They couldn't understand why I had to be given the option of flexibility while other women left their children with nannies or grandparents. It would not have made sense for me to work by paying for a full-time nanny and I didn't have the luxury of having Mother to take care of baby, like my sisters did.

I felt truly alone. Why was society like this—where the responsibility of childcare is solely the woman's? Why didn't workplaces understand the challenges a woman faces after giving birth? There was a total lack of empathy. I even had a friend tell me that her husband, who was in a senior position, didn't see the need to employ mums as there was no dearth of candidates. Given a choice, he or anyone else in his position would not choose a mum, however skilled she was. Was this the twenty-first century? It seemed as if we were still in the Stone Age.

Isn't it ironic—if women didn't give birth, where would the male workforce come from? Now I am not gender biased or one of those rabid feminists who believe that all men are trash—remember, I have a son. However, I would like to see everyone treated equally and have always felt so. Growing up in India, girls were not allowed to go out after dark while boys were. Why? Because the girls faced danger from men. Am I the only one to see the humour in this? We still have to go a long way to achieve equality, although there has been some progress in current times. Still, the onus of being safe is on the woman. We have to be careful. We have to stay home after dark. We have to wear appropriate clothes so as not to attract the male gaze. Men can do any damn thing they want. It is women who wear the burden of patriarchy.

Anyway, in the tug of war between the marriage and the job, there was an unsaid ultimatum. I sensed that my job was in danger and it proved to be true. I had no choice but to opt out of working. My employer was very unhappy (obviously) to lose me but wished me all the best for my future. A week after handing in my notice, I approached my manager about changing my mind and was told that this would disrupt all her plans. I accept she had a job to do, but was that the real reason? She hid behind the story that a senior manager in the location I worked in was behind this and that she had no influence over the matter. I wonder how it would have worked if the roles were reversed?

I would not have loved my child less if I was working, yet I gave up the position I had worked hard to get to—it was the beginning of falling behind in my career progression. I fell back into the routine of being a full-time mum. I would be lying if I said I didn't feel resentful. My career had changed me and I had tasted the glorious fruits of being independent. I loved being a working woman. I had tasted the fruits of success and it had given me a much-needed boost of self-confidence. Yes, working had restored my sense of self and shaped me into a woman who was grounded and proud of who she was. But now, that lay shattered like a broken vase.

I wanted to send my son to a private school and with two wages, we could have done so. That opportunity was now lost. I started having mood swings, feeling low and angry. I felt unsupported by my husband, the person I had trusted and whose child I had borne. He and his family suggested that I was suffering from post-natal depression. Since I still trusted him, I got medical advice, which resulted in a referral for counselling. I was looking for answers, which the counsellors could not provide. They were trained to listen. However, I got tired of talking and of the one-sided nature of the sessions. Once the counsellor also told me that the romantic view of marriage that we are often fed is far from the truth. Was it though?

At that time, I didn't have the voice or courage to speak up about my childhood trauma to a stranger. In fact, I had never talked about my childhood, after that awful time when I had failed to receive support and empathy from the friends I had opened up to during my university days. A therapist I saw later told me that childbirth can bring up emotions from childhood and affect one's mental well-being. And in my case, the issue I had was a huge burden to carry around. When she said this, it touched my heart. She was full of admiration for the way I carried myself and the strength I showed in not falling off the trail. This is something I would love to hear from Mother, but then coming from where she does—a society steeped in patriarchy and tradition—she could never understand my angst or my trauma. She stills tells me that I should have become a doctor. For what? To save lives? Yes, I can take that but not just for the sake of the money. Thanks to my successful career, I was able to provide financial help to rebuild her house and help my sisters when they faced financial emergencies.

I was fortunate to be offered a part-time job, five minutes from home, by a business acquaintance who rated me well for my skills and intelligence. It was to cover another staff member's maternity leave and she asked me to pick the hours and days I would like. Of course, my husband was not happy, but this was something I sorely needed for my own mental well-being and, with the doctors having said the same, he couldn't disagree. Our son was very well looked after by a childminder in her home on the days I worked, and he thrived. So, once this job ended, I took up other part-time local jobs. They were not as highly paid as the city jobs, but they helped me to keep my skills relevant, gave me exposure to hands-on work, and were a great confidence booster.

However, my marriage was not in a good place and was deteriorating with every passing day. This could have been due to us living apart or our differences coming to the surface. Externally everything looked good—we had a comfortable house and car, a lovely boy, and we were still going on exotic holidays. But there was resentment from both sides, and I found it hard to conceal my bitterness. Growing up, I had never had any guidance in being able to handle situations calmly. I came from a hot-headed, emotionally strung family. The counselling I went for never reached the core of my issues. I was left an emotional wreck. I veered between sadness and anger. I didn't know how to express myself and it came out as rage, especially when I felt I was not understood, which also served as a provocation.

My husband had no idea how to support me or deal with me. On one level, it was not his fault. He just blamed me, calling me hot-tempered and selfish. This made a bad situation even worse. Thinking that I was on the verge of a mental breakdown, he gave up his job, which in any case he never liked. Now the pressure began to build up even further. I had enough and more to deal with and the financial insecurity drove me further up the wall. It was a conundrum that we couldn't get ourselves out of. I desperately wanted to tell my mother or sisters about what was happening in the hope that they would understand. But how could I when I myself didn't know what was wrong with me. Everything was churning within me and my mind was like a tornado, twisted with a deluge of conflicting thoughts and emotions. I wondered, was everything really my shortcoming? It didn't help that my husband said that I didn't have support from my family as they knew how bad I was. It was then that I told him what had happened to me in my childhood and how I never had any support then, when it mattered most.

You cannot stop a storm or a volcano from erupting; they are forces of nature. The unhappiness, the blame, the shame, the guilt, the trauma and everything else that was bubbling within me surfaced and the husband and I had a major showdown. My husband behaved disrespectfully towards me and I would not have it. I took steps to get support from the community, which he didn't like. In the meantime, he told his family about my ordeal at the hands of a family member. I don't believe they understood the enormity and trauma of what I had been through and how it had affected me. I forgive them for saying that it was my fault and that it was due to my 'loose' character that I had faced the abuse. As if a child of four (by then my son was of this age) could defend herself or invite a sexual encounter. Even as I was facing the abuse while growing up, it had *never* been consensual, and I was underage for the entirety of it.

They asked me to speak to a family friend, who was a well-known psychiatrist. This is something I regret to this day. It was almost like falling into a trap. I don't think they did it purposely. But I had so hoped to find support and answers, but it was not to be so. I had hoped that speaking to the psychiatrist would help quiet the demons of my past, give me some kind of closure, cleanse my soul, and help me move on. However, instead, I was deemed to be damaged beyond repair, as if I was made of metal, as if I was not an equal, as if I was not a flesh and blood human being. I was a mother, a good one too, and I had proved myself in my career and by being a contributing member to society. But now, I was looked upon as damaged goods…

Chapter 18
It Takes Two to Tango

I had this gut feeling that things were not going to be easy and it broke my heart when I looked at the innocent face of my darling child. I would do anything in my power to save him from any sadness. But power was what I lacked because it was not just down to me—it takes two to tango, as the saying goes. I was bereft of love in the marriage, but I was willing to carry on for the sake of my son. It was in the early years of his life that I started feeling helpless. And these feelings gave rise to despair and anger. I begged my husband to try to make it work and to forgive me for whatever he felt I had wronged him for. There were accusations and allegations made against me by him, which drove his family away from me.

I felt isolated and cut off. Gone were the days when I would have endless chats with his mother or my sisters-in-law. I was lucky that I had a couple of close friends who stood by me, who believed in me and brought out my strength and kept me going. My family in India had no say in all of this; neither did they offer any emotional support. They just asked me to do whatever I saw as best because they had no idea as to how they could be of any help in these fraught circumstances. This led my husband to hurt me further. He taunted me by saying that even my family didn't back me. By then, I had had enough of being treated like a villain. And for what? For wanting to follow my dreams, my career, and contributing to the household?

My name was left off wedding invitations and I was not included in family get-togethers. I was heartlessly pushed off from the pedestal his family had put me on. Why could they not see my pain, my loneliness? They were punishing my 'bad behaviour', as they would put it. Everything came to light when I received a letter from his solicitors saying that the marriage had broken down irretrievably and hence we needed to work out the custody of our child. The letter came close to my birthday. I was in a state of shock; I was literally blindsided. Like me, my friends couldn't believe he could have done something like this. When I met my friends for dinner, I took the letter along to show it to them. In the meanwhile, my husband and I were still living in the same house that we owned and still shared a bank account. But he never thought it fit to inform me that he was going to fight me custody of our son.

I thank God for giving me the wisdom to get back to full-time work so I would have an income to support myself and my child. I took advice from lawyers on the back of the letter I had received and filed for divorce. I felt automated on one level, yet overly emotional.

Everything we had built together had come to naught. And we had to fight for the child we both loved and adored— the reason we had carried on with the marriage. I cursed myself for not having taken up his offer for a trial separation when I was still breastfeeding my son. There was no way he could snatch the child from my bosom then.

The bank accounts were split. I had nothing to my name, as I always put everything I earned into the joint account. The house was put up for sale… the house where our child had started his life. There were so many memories tied to it. In spite of being in a loveless marriage, the love and joy my son had brought into my life had permeated the house and it still carried those bittersweet memories of cherished times I had shared with him, his milestones, and the simple joys of taking care of him.

But it was not our home any longer as there was no longer any love for each other in our marriage. While all this was happening, we also had to work out who would get custody of our child. There was a lot of paperwork to go through and my head was swimming with the information overload. By then I had found a full-time job in the city, which helped me pay my solicitor's stiff bills. I was on my own, but due to the fact that I was earning well, I could get no help with legal fees and or any tax relief.

The whole process was like a rollercoaster ride and I was running from pillar to post to fulfil all the procedures that were required. My husband, as mentioned earlier, had left his job and had started putting extra pressure on me to sell the house or face repossession due to non-payment of the mortgage. He started putting everything on his credit card, half of which I had to pay when we split everything fifty-fifty once the house was sold. In fact, if I had done the calculations, if I'd had the will to go through all that, I realize that I ended up paying for his sports tickets and other impulsive expenses, which I had not partaken of. I wanted to give him a chance to start over. I can't vouch that he felt the same. On the contrary, he preferred to see me struggle and suffer since he believed that it was all my fault and that I should be punished for the same. Oh yes, until today he blames it all on me and is still bitter and full of hatred towards me.

I am no saint in this matter and I do get frustrated with him even now, losing my cool, which I regret later. But my spiritual leader told me that the best thing to do was to let go and send him good vibes. I can in all honesty say that I have never wished him ill. Things didn't work out between us, but he is the father of my child. I grew up without a father's love and guidance; I didn't want my son to have to face the same. So, when it came to deciding on custody during an out-of-court consultation, I agreed to co-parent our child with his father. This meant that our son would spend fifty percent of his time with each of us and we would pay for his care as per this split. The law of the land had no alimony or any other allowance for me, even though I was the lower earner by virtue of our professions.

The day I had to move out of the house, my son stayed with me. I had a couple of friends come to help me settle into a rented apartment I had found at the last minute. My husband had already found a place for himself and kept putting pressure on me to sell the house fast. I had nowhere to go, and had I not found a home in time for me and my child, I would have lost out on the joint custody arrangement. I had married such a conniving and cruel man—something I never ever thought would happen. Had I worn blinkers all through my marriage? Or had he always been this cunning that he kept this cruel side of him hidden from me?

The furniture was split between us so we could fit it into our respective rented accommodations. The first night was the hardest. I had to pretend that everything was normal and stay strong for my son. He needed me and I had a great responsibility to live up to his expectations and make him feel loved and secure. I couldn't sleep that night. When morning arrived, my son lifted my spirits by saying, "It feel like home, Mummy." I remember it to this day. It made me feel all warm and fuzzy, and suddenly the horizon didn't look dark and gloomy. There was a silver lining of hope.

While all this was happening and my life was being turned upside down, I never heard from my sisters and rarely from Mother. This was before the time of WhatsApp calls. International calls were expensive in those days. Whilst Mother had always persuaded me to call them when they faced any difficulties or had a reason for celebration, I was bereft that she never asked my sisters to return the gesture. And neither did she reach out to me at a time when my life was falling apart. I have always cared about not hurting others and even as I write this, I feel a sense of guilt. But write I must; there is no hiding anything now.

My husband was not content with the out-of-court decision and called me to court for a hearing on the custody. He fought for full custody on the basis of my mental health and that he was in a better position to look after our son as he had his family in this country. I upheld my integrity and dignity. I wasn't going to stoop to his level. I got letters of reference from family, friends, and employers to prove who I was, which I submitted in my statement to the court. The court case turned out to be extravagantly expensive, although it ended up with the same ruling of joint custody. Please don't laugh out loud, but as absurd as it may sound, my husband blamed me for making him bankrupt. I pity him for his childish behaviour.

I went into the courtroom on my own, while he was accompanied by his brother and his barrister. The judge was elderly and wise, no surprise there. He was very appreciative of my education and background. He ruled out sole custody for the father, saying that he simply couldn't take the child away from the mother. On my request, the judge asked his barrister to make our son's passport available to me. Without my knowledge, my husband had taken the passport from the safe and hidden it away. This was against the law and was treated as abuse of power.

It was hard, but I do not know where I found the will not to give up. Work, looking after my son, the court case, and the entire mental and emotional trauma was taking a toll on me. I didn't feel hungry, but I would cook for my son and eat the leftovers. At work, colleagues would ask me to join them to get a bite to eat, but I was never interested. I lost a lot of weight. One day, at work, I had a blackout and ended up in accident and emergency. As I had no family to call upon, two of my colleagues waited for me while I was checked out—an act of kindness I will never forget. From there on, I had to go through a series of check-ups. When I went to see a cardiologist, she told me that I was working in flight and fight mode and that it was no wonder that my health was deteriorating. Clutching at straws, I almost told her about my ordeal, but I couldn't bring myself to do so. I didn't want to ruin her image of me—the image of a strong, responsible mum and employee. I didn't want to appear broken in spite of whatever I had been dealt with.

My single colleagues at work were going onto dating sites, looking for love and companionship. They urged me to sign up. I, however, was very confused, because while going through the divorce and custody process, I had got close to my current partner. We had never intended to, but we fell in love. It was a sticky situation, as he was not single. I couldn't see any light at the end of this black, very black tunnel, I had little hope in finding fulfilment in this love relationship. I felt secure yet very insecure. Back in India, Mother and my sisters were trying to find a match for me. They could not comprehend that I would never leave the UK, because it would mean forsaking the joint custody of my son. Nothing meant more to me than my beautiful boy.

I concentrated on building my life and next, I bought a home for my son and me. My very own apartment—the happiest home I have ever lived in. It was as if I was working on autopilot, going through the motions of life. I lived and looked forward to the days I had my son with me. It was not easy, but I did it. I took help from friends in emergencies and was lucky to find very reliable wraparound childcare for him. At school, my son would unselfconsciously tell his teachers that he lived in two homes. By then, he had given up on the idea that his parents would live together again, an idea that was reinforced when I bought the new house. He knew that there was no turning back now. That chapter in his life was closed. Mummy and Daddy would never reunite…

Chapter 19
Reverberations...

My personal life may have hit rock bottom. Thankfully, in my professional life, it was the opposite. At that time, the industry I work in was going through a major transformation. The lows in my personal life were compensated by the highs in my professional life, where I was soaring to newer heights and enjoying the delectable fruits of success. I enjoyed being in the forefront of the progress in digital technology. The proliferation of smartphones and devices, the growth of social media platforms, and an increase is media streaming gave rise to new ways of working and living over the years. I decided to take up the opportunity to work away from the city. It did mean opting out of being a part of the rat race, but it did allow me to enjoy quality time with my son.

I was used to change, wasn't I? I had moved from a small town, survived in a big city, started life in a new country, and not only got through but overcome all the challenges that life had lobbed me with. So, when I was asked at an interview why I had changed so many (far too many) jobs, I didn't allow that to dampen my spirits.

In fact, I felt odd that the person interviewing me had never moved from the town they were born in and had been in the same job from when they had started working. It's not that I find anything wrong in that. It's just that I also feel there is nothing wrong in having made several career moves. For someone like me, it was about adapting and enduring. Life is never static. It is all about change. And, for some people, that change comes at a heavy price. That change is forced by circumstances. Wrought by the ever-changing curveballs that life throws at you. For me, many a time, change was not something I had sought; change had been forced on me.

In an earlier chapter, I had said that we have the strength within us to carry on. There are times when we all feel weak or feel the need for reassurance and support. I have done exactly that. I have reached out for support, picked myself up, and carried on. Even when, at one of my jobs, I faced sexual harassment from a woman. This time I did not want history to repeat itself; I did not want to keep quiet. So, I stood up for myself and for others in my workplace. I took up my case with the company's management. They were empathetic and appeared to be shocked, yet they couldn't support me in raising an inquiry, as I had no proof. She had come onto me during a company party and the restaurant where it was held was shut down due to an accident. As luck or misfortune would have it, there was no CCTV camera footage that would have proved my case. She got lucky, while I and several others got plain unlucky. Nevertheless, I did report the matter to the police, so it went on her record, should she victimise anyone else.

Over time, in the developed world, harassment of any form—especially sexual harassment—is being taken very seriously. No longer is it all right for casting directors to invite young aspirants to the couch. Or to expect the woman at a meeting to make the tea or order lunch or snacks. However, the key to an evolved world lies in embracing the diversity of colleagues and citizens and making everyone feel included, no matter who they are and where they are from. There is a lot of work still needed for this feeling of respect and comradeship to become second nature. Social media has helped in spreading this cause, but not without causing harm, as there are strong opinions held by both sides and, with the extensive reach that social media has, these opinions can go viral in no time. While social media's reach is a huge advantage, it can be a toxic weapon when it is used to spread prejudices, racism, sexism, patriarchy, religious hatred, and other biases.

I'm forever concerned about my son falling into the wrong hands while he is innocently playing games online. I've drilled it into him to be very careful about who he interacts with and what details he shares, to the point that he has become quite cynical. I taught him early on that only a doctor or nurse is allowed to see and touch him for medical reasons, that too in the presence of his parents. And that should he have any doubts or questions, he can come to me or his father without any hesitation or fear and that he can trust us to protect and listen to him. I have made sure to teach him about 'bad touch' and 'good touch'. I never want him to go through what I went through. And I want him to know that his parents will always stand by him and do whatever we can to protect and safeguard him. I know the hurt of having no one in your corner, of navigating abuse as a young, innocent child. That pain still lingers within me.

I was worried about having a new life partner. I could not bring a stranger home to my son. He was already adjusting to a new life where his parents were living apart. His cosy little life had been turned upside down. Now, my son and I had started afresh in a new home and we were happy and at peace. I was scared to disrupt his life all over again and change the dynamics of our relationship.

From the first time I met my current partner, I knew I could trust him. Once, when we used to work together, there was someone bothering me. It felt completely natural for me to go to my partner, who was a colleague then, and I requested him to walk back with me to the lobby from the banquet hall. I also used to trust him to give me feedback before I gave any presentation before hundreds of people. I felt like myself, confident and fearless, in his presence. We had something special, an instant chemistry and we fell deeply in love. It was not intentional, although I do feel remorse for the hurt that our relationship caused to his near and dear ones. I also have no justification or excuses to make for the raised eyebrows of society or for their judgmental outlook. It was something that happened, a result of the deep love we felt for each other.

It was not smooth sailing though; in fact, it was a very rough ride. I was overcoming the aftermath of the divorce, facing up to society, feeling the need to explain myself, etcetera. I had not even scratched the surface when it came to finding closure for what had happened in my childhood. I used to get upset and have misunderstandings with my partner, even though I loved him so much. I feared losing him because of my mood swings and anger, and it didn't help that I was being badgered by my ex-husband, who seemed to have a lot of anger within him.

I had to rediscover myself. It should not have been difficult, as all I needed to do was to believe in who my partner said I was. Later on, I'd find my therapist talking about how I was so hard on myself. She worked with me to get me to believe in my positive attributes—the very same ones, I realised, that my partner had been always pointing out to me every day.

They say children are innocent and can see the good from the bad. From when we have been together and even today, my son tells my partner that he is happy in the knowledge that I have someone to look after me when he is with his dad. That makes me laugh out loud as, when he is with me, I fondly call myself his slave, as I am constantly at his beck and call or lose sleep on the days he is not well. I am not complaining. I love having my son with me and I would do anything for him. I am so content these days because my partner and son have formed a bond of their own. What makes me especially happy is that my son trusts him and opens up to him about all kinds of things. So much so that when I do the school pick-up and drop-off he is often silent or busy on his phone, but with my partner he will talk nonstop.

You will be surprised to know that my mother—who wanted me to get married only to a boy from my own caste—is fine with me being unmarried and cohabiting with a man who is not from my religion. It took time for her to see the truth and the good in him. When she met him, she embraced him with open arms and huge smiles, instantly approving of his clean-cut looks, height, and dress sense. I had not expected her to accept him so easily. It was a bigger surprise for me when she told me that, had we lived in India, she would live with us. She cannot move here, as the UK is very cold, and she will be lonely without her near and dear ones and my siblings. Also, she is not fluent in English, which makes it even tougher for her.

My sisters and friends (only the Indian girls) ask me how it is to live with a *Gora* (white skin). My simple smile in response to this says it all. They can see the change in me through the years. I've become so much calmer. If I could, I would express how it feels to be in love and know love. Sorry to sound mushy, but I really mean it. I've found my soul mate, someone with whom

I can share everything—the good and the bad. We can spend hours in each other's company, we are attuned to each other's needs, and we laugh at each other's silly jokes. He has accepted me and loves me for who I am. After all that I've been through, that is what is so special—to be loved unconditionally. Thankfully, he makes no fuss about food or how long I take to decide on a dress or when I continue shopping for hours after telling him that this is the last shop. We enjoy traveling as a family or just the two of us, and have been lucky to take city breaks, beach holidays, and ski trips over the years. He is always in trouble when he has to take photos of me, as I reject most of them; it's so easy to do so on a smartphone—I can delete them instantaneously. In spite of that, he will indulge me and take photos and selfies. Yes, I love him. I love our little unit of three. It's the simple joys that make life worth living. With my partner in my life, I've found love, peace, and fulfilment. Life has come a full circle.

Chapter 20
To New Beginnings

I started writing this book with the aim of finding closure and sharing my experiences in the hope that someone would find it helpful. Although I am still not sure if or how I'll publish it. What if it's a failure? Or, worse still, what will the family say about me exposing the dark, dirty secret? I get nightmares about falling out with my family, being cut off by everyone, the perpetrator being taken to the police, and getting out scot-free after paying a fat bribe. Will they understand that part of the reason that I have decided to come out and speak the truth of my life is to forgive, let go, move on... But then, does it even matter?

I have a tendency to be hard on myself when something goes wrong or if I make a mistake at work. I fail to see the other side until it is pointed out to me. I have set very high standards for myself and when I fail to achieve them, I believe everyone is better than me and I have no level playing field to stand on.

I have gone on my own journey of forgiveness—finding myself and my purpose. It has taken me the best part of two and half years to bare it all. During this time, a lot has happened. Time stands still for no one…

My son was diagnosed with a neurodevelopment condition. No parent would like their child to have any condition. However, I am at peace, knowing that he is not worse off in any way and that there is a great deal of support from his school and the community. I'm also thankful that I can support him in the right way. His dad had put down some of his behaviour to being naughty, overly emotional, or even blaming it on me (the easy explanation, right?). My son does have some of my traits for sure. He is a bright boy and his thinking, like mine, is very black and white with very few shades of grey in between. He is also very attached to me. Since he is so similar to me, I went through a screening for the same condition (much to my doctor's disbelief! Nonetheless, she did support me in my endeavour). However, the result was negative.

Then came the Covid-19 pandemic, changing the way we live, work, and travel and, sadly, causing chaos to economies around the globe. So many have lost their jobs; students have had to stay away from their educational institutions, while those starting off on careers to fulfil their dreams and ambitions have been left in a void. Health care professionals have taken the place of God on Earth, helping the sick while putting themselves at risk. Politicians and governments are grappling to find a solution to this chaos, extending financial support (in some countries), while scientists have worked day and night to find a vaccine.

Due to the isolation people experienced during the lockdown and the fear of the known and unknown, there is a huge and long-lasting effect on the mental health of citizens of all ages. Countries which have a robust network of support for mental health are struggling to keep up with the demand. My thoughts go out to those who have no support. Whatever may be the case, mental health is still a stigma. Say you break a bone and need to take leave of absence from work, you can be open about it. You'll also get the sympathy and empathy of your colleagues. But when you need time off to recover from a mental health breakdown, it's a hush-hush matter.

I've been condemned by my mother for taking treatment for my mental health. She believes that it is wrong of doctors to prescribe psychiatric medications as they have a negative impact, while she will happily pop pills for her aches and pains. For her, what society says matters more than her daughter's mental well-being, because she doesn't want anyone to know that I am undergoing therapy. In India, a vast majority still believe that those undergoing therapy are either mad or weak.

I posed the question to a friend, an experienced psychiatrist. The analogy (which made perfect sense) I was given was that when we get an infection, we will not go without antibiotics, so why would we not treat a condition that affects us mentally? Just as infections that are left untreated can cause damage to our bodies, mental issues can have a marked impact on our health. So, is it about education or awareness or is it about removing the stigma? I don't believe there is a simple, straightforward answer. It is a combination of all three. But society as a whole needs to be more aware, accepting, and empathetic towards mental health issues.

I decided to make my own contribution to this cause, with the hope of supporting myself and others who face or have faced a similar situation. I set up a meeting with two of my senior leaders, where I told them that I was undergoing treatment for depression. I also opened up about the root cause of it—the sexual abuse I faced during my formative years. They were sympathetic and commended me on my bravery for speaking up. I also told the HR department, who agreed that there was nothing to hide; they told me that the company supports such causes. I would like to put my trust in the company's support in equality, because I do not want to face any negative consequences that will affect the progress of my career. As a woman and a senior member of the company, I took a stand and I am happy and proud that I did so. If we don't stand up for ourselves and our causes, who will? I do believe that we are our own best advocates.

I heard a famous personality who is a supporter of mental health say, "The worst thing you can do is being depressed about depression." I have stopped hiding my depression. I live with it and intend to come out of it. I am lucky to have the best care and access to professionals. I no longer tell my son that I am going for physiotherapy when I go for my psychotherapy. There is no shame in it. He should not see this as a stigma, as he is a torchbearer of the future. I am waiting for him to reach adulthood to let him know what happened to me as a child, and he knows that he is not allowed to read this book until then. He has asked me to print at least one copy for myself.

His father told me that my son feels sorry for me as he knows of my depression. While it very disparaging and disheartening to hear this, I forgive my ex for this and for everything else I expected from him and that he could not provide. He is not a bad person. He loves his son but is very set in his own ways. I have never wished him ill and never will. I do sometimes long for the times I spent with his mother—the only person, my son says, from his dad's side of the family who has ever asked about how I am.

I thought I had to be someone else to be rid of my negative thoughts, my anxieties, and being overly sensitive. I fought against myself, and that was obviously not the right thing to do. I am taking a different approach now—to believe in myself, to appreciate who I am, and work with that. I did say that this is a journey and that there are no shortcuts. Sometimes, I have had to travel the same path over and over again. Depression doesn't magically disappear overnight. There are good days and bad days; there are times when you feel that the darkness will never go; there are other days when there is a sliver of hope; there are other days when the sun is shining and you feel that everything is all right with the world. It's a roller-coaster ride and I hope that one day, I'm able to step off it.

Nature and nurture play important roles, as is evident in my case. Living outside of India, I have noticed the difference. I was brought up to be God fearing—*do this and something bad will happen, eat this and you will be sick*. There is nothing like that. God doesn't judge us. It is human nature to judge and it is human beings who judge, and it is we who put chains on ourselves and others. We can eat what we want and be who we want. As long as we are kind and compassionate and do not harm others.

My therapist asked me to value whatever I achieve or do, however small or big—like cooking a meal for the family, bringing up my son to be a good citizen, being a diligent employee, a caring neighbour, a loving friend, an adoring partner, the list goes on... And that has really helped me to appreciate even the small things in life. It's a slow process and I am taking it step by step. But each achievement helps me to feel good about myself. It instils confidence in me and gives me hope and inspiration to better myself and do things I never would have dreamt of doing earlier.

This book is an example of that. Writing it has been far from easy. I was filled with self-doubt (an enduring gift from my childhood). Dredging up all those awful memories from the past and having to relive them has been traumatising. There were months when I couldn't write because I was so overcome with self-doubt, grief, and pain. Sometimes I dreaded putting the words down on paper, as it would make it all real again. And there were times that I couldn't find a way to express what I wanted.

But now, I have finally finished the book. I overcame all the overarching anguish and the lack of self-confidence to create something meaningful. It has helped me discover my true self and also helped me to come to terms with my past. The slate is clean now, although the trauma will always remain hidden somewhere deep below. But my greatest learning from my journey has been this—*what happened to me was not my fault.* I was a victim of circumstances. I was a victim of patriarchy. And I was a victim of a heartless, cruel, lecherous vulture.

So today, I stand a more confident and self-realised individual. I have a deep, abiding assurance within me. What he did to me and the repercussions that I bear do not define me. I choose to define myself and who I am. He has *not* won, I *have*.

My journey continues. The Me Too movement has changed the meaning of the words 'me too'. It has given scores of women across the globe the courage to come out and tell their stories of sexual abuse. So many predators are now behind bars or have lost their jobs and their reputations. And here is this book, my 'me too' offering… from me to you…